Emma Speaks Out

Life and Writings of
Emma Molloy (1839-1907)

Martha M. Pickrell

Guild Press
Carmel, Indiana

ISBN 1-57860-073-1

Library of Congress No. 99-71526

CONTENTS

PREFACE AND ACKNOWLEDGEMENTS

How does a woman find success, fulfillment, and acceptance in her work? How does she give sufficient attention to both her work and her family?

When her career presents different types of opportunities, what choices does she make? When those opportunities lead her into new places and situations, how does she cope with the changes this inevitably brings?

And if her role is a public one, how does she deal with the responses that public figures so often arouse?

A century ago and more, Emma Molloy of Indiana, a pioneering journalist, public speaker, reformer, and evangelist, faced these questions in her own unique way, with few examples to guide her. Today largely forgotten, once she was fairly well-known, and her activities were wide-ranging, taking her well beyond Indiana and at times onto the national stage.

My own first discovery of Emma Molloy came in the 1960s and 1970s, when I read her vibrant, strongly opinionated writings in the *South Bend National Union* and *Elkhart Observer,* her long obituary in the *South Bend Times,* and her flowery biography in a now-rare volume, James M. Hiatt's *The Ribbon Workers.* I shared my early research in a newspaper article.[1]

But I knew I had not done Emma's story justice, and that there was much more to discover. Two events—two people—inspired me to go further. My former teacher, Tom Vander Ven, Professor of English at Indiana University South Bend, created a fascinating drama, *Three Women: An Indiana Medley,* based partly on Emma's story. And my sister-in-law, Marlene Deahl Merrill, an historian based at Oberlin College, discovered Emma's writings and speeches in the national woman suffrage weekly, the *Woman's Journal.*

And so, in the late 1980s, I headed an Emma Molloy research

project. Much-appreciated help came from Indiana University South Bend, which arranged the project and offered affiliate scholar privileges; from the Martin and Beardsley foundations of Elkhart, which supplied funds; from a number of scholars and fellow researchers; and from over 150 libraries and archives in twenty-three states, Canada, and England.

The hundreds of items that were discovered have been organized into a series of "scrapbooks" documenting Emma's life, family and career, much as she herself, or a family member or friend, might have created. Copies of this multi-volume research collection have been donated to the archives of the Northern Indiana Historical Society in South Bend and to the Indiana Historical Society Library in Indianapolis.

The narrative that follows draws upon the project research and began as a talk written for the Indiana Historical Society's annual conference in 1989. Since almost no personal papers were found, and for other reasons, I did not write the long biography I had originally planned. This more modest work has the advantage of having room for a good sampling of Emma's writings and speeches.

It is my hope that it will provide a starting point for more research and writing. As will become apparent to my readers, there are many "leads" still to be followed up, connections to be discovered, mysteries to be solved, gaps to be filled, conclusions to be reached. There is much more, in fact, to be drawn from the material that has been collected.

Many thanks are due. Among the researchers and scholars, I wish to thank especially Richard Dupuis, who thoroughly documented Emma's activities in England; Joyce Burgess, who researched her early life in South Bend; J. Barrett Guthrie in San Juan Capistrano, California, who provided important family information; Professor David Fahey at Miami University of Ohio, who gave guidance on temperance history; and Mary Alice Pacey in Washington, Kansas, Mary C. Martin in Madison, Wisconsin, and Eileen Martin in Port Townsend, Washington, who provided vital details on Emma's far-extended life.

Among others who were of help were Laureen Bostedt and Jeanne

Denham in South Bend, Don Hoak in Elkhart, Martin F. Barlag in LaPorte, Nancy Weems in Montgomery, Alabama, Louise Marsh in Madison, Wisconsin, Elizabeth F. Moe in McGregor, Iowa, Professor Hugh Denney in Columbia, Missouri, Brad Gernand in Norman, Oklahoma, Pearl R. Jones in Baker City, Oregon, and Jean Hass in Creswell, Oregon.

Among librarians and archivists, I wish to thank especially those at the Elkhart Public Library and the Schurz Library at Indiana University South Bend. I also worked closely with the Northern Indiana Historical Society and St. Joseph County Public Library in South Bend; Elkhart County Historical Society in Bristol; Methodist archives in South Bend and Elkhart; Mishawaka-Penn Public Library; LaPorte Public Library; Allen County Public Library, Fort Wayne; Indiana State Library and Indiana Historical Society, Indianapolis; Indiana WCTU, Knightstown; Earlham College Archives, Richmond; Frances E. Willard Memorial Library and United Library at Garrett Theological Seminary, both in Evanston, Illinois; Elgin, Illinois, Public Library; State Historical Society of Wisconsin, Madison; Neal Dow Memorial, Portland, Maine; Boston Public Library; American Antiquarian Society, Worcester; Stanton/Anthony Project, University of Massachusetts, Amherst; Alabama Department of Archives and History, Montgomery; Kansas State Historical Society, Topeka; University of Kansas Library, Lawrence; Washington County Historical Society, Washington, Kansas; State Historical Society of Missouri, Columbia; Oklahoma Historical Society, Oklahoma City; University of Oklahoma Library, Norman; and the British Library, among others.

Thanks to Daniel Merrill and Marlene Deahl Merrill, to Professors Vander Ven, Patrick Furlong, Patricia McNeal and Donald Marti, and to Margaret Emery, for reading my drafts and giving useful guidance, and to Professor Lester Lamon for shepherding the project.

This book is lovingly dedicated to the memory of my husband, Bob Pickrell, who spent hundreds of hours at his computer creating an invaluable index to the "Emma Molloy Research Collection," and offered unfailing encouragement and support.

A NOTE ON NAMES

During her lifetime, Emma was known by a number of distinct names, as well as adopting pseudonyms from time to time as a writer.

Born Emily F. Barrett, at some point she became known as Emma, and some of her very early writings are signed "Emma F. Barrett." Her middle name has not been found. Her first married name, as she used it in her writings, was Emma F. Pradt (1858-1867). Her second married name, the name under which she became prominent in the fields of journalism, temperance and woman's rights, was Emma Molloy (1867-89).

Her third and final married name, since she married a Barrett, was Emma Molloy Barrett (1889-1907). Under this name, often abbreviated to Mrs. E. M. Barrett, sometimes hyphenated as Mrs. Emma Molloy-Barrett, she worked as an evangelist on the West coast.

But Emma Molloy dominates this book, because this was the name under which she was best known, and because the story I have to tell dwells most on her Emma Molloy years. In my earlier article I used the name Emma *Barrett* Molloy, since it includes her own family origins as well. However, she herself did not use this combination of names, nor did any of her contemporaries in writing about her. In the text, I have used whatever name was hers at the period, but often simply "Emma."

Pseudonyms I feel confident in identifying as hers include "Nellie More," "B. E. F.," "Polly Wiggins" and "Polly Quiggle," "Mabel Clare," "Anna Maria Stubbs," "Emma F. P.," "Eliza S. Pratt," "Mrs. Pat Molloy," "Mrs. Petroleum V. Nasby," "Belle Beach," "Aunt Polly," "Aunt Nabby," "E.," and "M. S.," and very likely, "M. E. E." Other possibilities include "Lily Lea," "L. A. Kingsbury," "Anon.," "Emma Eggleson," "Lizzie," and "Millicent Lee."

Emma Molloy, c. 1876-77. Emma distributed copies of this photograph in her lecturing career. She wrote on one, to a friend in South Bend, "April 1, 1877. Faithful to the End. Emma Molloy." This phrase expressed her deep dedication to her temperance work.

PART I: LIFE

1
A STRONG-MINDED WOMAN

In 1870 Emma Molloy of South Bend was thirty years old and truly enjoying her pioneering role as the first and only woman newspaper editor in northern Indiana.[1] As co-editor, or "editress," of the weekly *South Bend National Union* with her second husband, Edward Molloy, she had become adept at nearly every aspect of journalism. And she wrote often about the issues which concerned her, especially those of the advancement and self-respect of women.

A small, energetic woman with large, expressive eyes, she was far from any Victorian stereotype. As active as any modern woman, she was often out around town or in nearby communities, gathering news and stories of interest, soliciting funds, and visiting the offices of her fellow editors.

In addition to her household duties, she put in long days writing, proofreading, and dealing with office problems. On occasion, she had even spent long nights setting type. On top of all this, she had begun to give talks on the subject of women's rights. And—she was pregnant!

Eight years later, billed as America's foremost female temperance advocate, she would speak from a stage in London to a large audience of men and women about the need for laws prohibiting the sale and use of alcohol. A few years after that, she would make her way on foot across a frozen river in Oklahoma to deliver temperance sermons to the Cherokee Indians. And much later, during the time of the San Francisco earthquake, she would be evangelizing in California.

Throughout her life, despite suffering many sorrows and disappointments, and even scandal, and never possessing wealth, the self-reliant Emma Molloy would take full advantage of new opportunities opening for women, by developing and using her considerable talents for writing and public speaking.

As a persuasive journalist, temperance lecturer, evangelist, teacher, and personal counselor, she would influence the lives of hundreds of thousands of people. Often making courageous changes, sometimes making sacrifices in her personal life, she would contribute her share to the growing movements that fought for women's rights, temperance, and prison reform, and to the trend that brought more and more women into Christian ministry.

Her intensity always set her apart — an intensity of effort and caring, and an intensity of personal conviction that had its start in her Methodist upbringing in the pioneer village of South Bend. It was an optimistic faith, one that stressed the possibilities of improvement, reform, and salvation for all, despite an imperfect world. That the world was imperfect she learned very early.

2
YOUTH AND RESPONSIBILITY
1839-1858

Emily F. Barrett was born in South Bend, Indiana on July 17, 1839. Four years earlier, her parents, William Lovell Barrett and Harriett Newton Barrett, had come from central New York State to the new settlement on the St. Joseph River. William Barrett was a watchmaker by trade.

According to local sources, William and Harriett Barrett hadn't really *meant* to settle in South Bend, which in 1835 was just a village, a large clearing in the wilderness filled with makeshift buildings. They had simply stopped on their way west. But townspeople persuaded William that there was a need for his work, and that they should make their home in South Bend.

The Barretts were a long-lived clan, strong in body and in religious belief. On Sundays in earlier days, William Barrett's father, John Barrett, a farmer of Ossian, New York, had led his children on long walks through the woods to the Methodist meeting house, singing hymns as they went. Susannah Bosworth Barrett, William Barrett's mother, would live to be ninety-five.[1]

Now, soon after coming to South Bend, William and Harriett Barrett became active in the fledgling First Methodist Episcopal Church and the village's combined Protestant Sunday school. Harriett Barrett, an energetic young woman with an outgoing personality and the zeal of a missionary, balanced her husband with his quiet, meticulous attention to his watch business and jewelry store on Michigan Street.

According to later accounts, Harriett taught the "three R's" to children of the village on weekdays, as well as teaching moral lessons on the Sabbath. Her daughter would take lifelong inspiration from her work.[2]

Yet she had few if any conscious memories of her mother, since Harriett Newton Barrett died in May, 1841, two months before her daughter's second birthday. To know her better, that daughter appears to have saved, for many years, letters written by her mother.

The only one of three children to survive infancy, Emily, or Emma, as she came to be called, was boarded out to other homes for several years when her father went to Chicago to work as a watchmaker. Later sources described her intense and long-lasting feelings of loneliness and insecurity. However, she also developed an exceptional self-reliance.[3]

She did find a welcoming affection in the home of George and Martha Bryson, a couple in their fifties, and their daughter and son-in-law, Amanda and Ruben Burroughs. Here the basic patterns of Emma's life were set: work, study, prayer, and some time for play.

George Bryson, a "local preacher" for the Methodist district, provided another model of a life of usefulness and ministry. Despite being at least partially blind, he served small rural congregations between the visits of the itinerant minister, and farmed with the aid of a son.

Among Emma's home duties, as she grew out of early childhood, were caring for the Burroughs' babies, and reading to her "foster grandfather." She later wrote nostalgically about him in the *South Bend National Union:*

> *It almost seems as if we could hear his voice in prayer as we gathered around the family altar, or feel his kindly arm about us, as, when sitting upon his knee, we read to him, through the long summer hours . . . on the vine-clad porch of the little tree-embowered cottage near the banks of the lovely St. Joe.*[4]

Emma Barrett was a bright student. She attended the rudimentary district schools, as well as a small private school run by Sophia Bookstaver, where the children "studied with a will."[5]

At Sunday school, she and her fellow pupils found a large lending library, and the challenge of memorizing innumerable Bible verses. Stories in the *Sunday School Advocate* admonished them to have faith, to be good, to be of service to others—with great urgency, since, in that era, a child might die at any time, and eternal salvation was felt to be at stake. The death of one of the Burroughs children further drove this lesson home.[6]

Emma's life changed considerably in the early 1850s, when, as South Bend began to grow with the coming of the railroad, her father returned from Chicago. He had married again. Harriett Eaker Barrett, his second wife, was a native of Palestine, Darke County, Ohio, and, like William himself, a staunch member of the Methodist Church.

Resuming his South Bend life as jeweler, Methodist, Mason, and Democrat, well known for the high silk hat he wore no matter what the weather, William Barrett built a two-story frame house near the river on East Marion Street. Emma appears to have lived with them. In 1853 her half-sister, Zilpha ("Dee") was born, the first of a family of two girls and three boys.[7]

By her early teens, no doubt somewhat engulfed by her home life, with its inevitable chores and likely a difficult emotional adjustment, Emma had set her sights on becoming independent of her family and living a useful, purposeful life. Teaching school, as her own mother had done, had been virtually the only "acceptable" occupation for middle-class girls, and during her last years of formal schooling, she very practically prepared for teaching by serving as a "pupil teacher."[8]

At the same time, however, the growing success of women as writers was offering a new vision of female independence and influence to a whole generation of girls, despite the severe limitations on women's lives and rights in that era. In 1852 many in South Bend read and discussed Harriett Beecher Stowe's *Uncle Tom's Cabin*. Two years later, *Ruth Hall*, by the popular writer "Fanny Fern," which Emma is known to have read, was published. It showed how a woman could make a living by writing, and could say exactly what she thought. And popular novelists like Mrs. E.D.E.N. Southworth were creating girl heroines who brought about change in others.[9]

Emma developed her skills in writing and dramatic recitation at the grammar school and academy on west Washington Street. At fourteen, she won a prize for an essay, and performed in humorous literary scenes, including "The School Committee." At fifteen, she was praised for the brilliance of her writings, especially her essay on "Education."

The Methodist Sunday school also encouraged her in writing and performance. One winter, for the school's annual exercises, she produced and starred in "The Fairy Queen of Love." A special flair for the dramatic would later serve her well in a life filled with many "performances."[10]

At fifteen or sixteen, she made a clean break with her childhood by going into the countryside, away from South Bend, to teach a rural one-room school. She seems to have performed this arduous job with enthusiasm. And in the spring of 1856, she advertised the organization of a school for young children in South Bend.[11]

At around the same time, her first writings were published in South Bend's newspapers. Newspapers were just beginning their transformation from the old partisan political sheet, primarily of interest to men, to the general-interest paper that welcomed varied features, appealing also to female readers. Her poems appeared in the *St. Joseph County Forum*, and in early 1856 four stories entitled "Heart Histories" by "Nellie More" appeared in the *St. Joseph Valley Register*, a paper that had been founded by future Vice President Schuyler Colfax.

Like most female writers of her time, sixteen-year-old Emma Barrett used pseudonyms in order to freely express her thoughts and maximize the power of her words. In her "Heart Histories," "Nellie," in the guise of an older woman, sermonized on the ill effects of cold parents, of a mother who "never knew the meaning of the word affection," and of a father who was a "silent man of business, whose highest thought was money."

Lovingly protective toward a girl friend, she called many girls "mere painted dolls," whose life of socializing was "without end or aim." She wrote,

> *...the crying evil of woman's bondage would...in a measure be eradicated...if girls were taught a higher view of life, than merely appealing to the outward senses of man...*[12]

She lashed out at men who were disloyal in love, and at gossips who destroyed reputations. And, with the idea of a possible future marriage very likely much on her mind, she criticized parents who did not prepare their daughters to be competent housekeepers—or good mothers.

Though information is extremely sketchy, it appears that at seventeen, Emma took a bolder step toward independence by going for a few weeks or months to the deep South, most likely stopping at Montgomery, Alabama, where her older cousins, the brothers Milo and Morris Barrett, had founded a printing business. According to a later source, she taught school. She may also have attended a girls' "college."

In the South she witnessed the shocking sight of slaves being auctioned, and heard their unfamiliar songs. That year also, she began to send essays and poems under her own name to the *North Iowa Times* of McGregor, Iowa. She had earlier known its editor, A. P. Richardson, in South Bend.[13]

School teaching was the subject of one of her early published essays. Here she expressed a teacher's warm feelings toward her pupils, and her heavy sense of responsibility, not only for their reading and writing, but for their moral development:

> *School is out, and the little ones linger round the weary teacher to kiss her and bid her good-by. No rod or ferule is needed there, love has conquered those little hearts and each one is desirous of her approbation...through the vista of coming years she read each little one's future, and prays that in their memory she may be a green spot...Oh! teachers, be not yours a responsible station? Beware! in your hand is moulding a mind created to live as long as God shall live.*[14]

3
Marriage and Disillusionment
1858-1867

Emma Barrett's writings seem to indicate a number of close friendships. A few pieces, such as the "Heart Histories" and a poem in the *Forum* by "B.E.F.," may very well point to an early disappointment in love. Then somehow she met a journeyman printer from Wisconsin named Louis A. Pradt.

Now she surrendered her limited independence for the dream of married happiness—though in some of her writings she expressed a prematurely wise caution about such hopes. In April, 1858, in South Bend, at the age of eighteen, she married Louis Pradt, and went with him to Sheboygan, Wisconsin.[1]

Louis Pradt was about twenty-seven, the son of a physician and the younger brother of an Episcopal priest and educator, the Rev. John B. Pradt. Perhaps quite different from some of the young men she knew in South Bend, Louis had a talent for stage acting and a fondness for alcohol.

They must have had their share of happy times together. But as a young woman who had grown up on sermons against liquor, her experiences with his drinking were extremely traumatic. Her efforts to keep him from drinking failed, and the problem worsened over the course of their nine-year marriage. It also helped make her a bitter, lifelong foe of alcohol.[2]

They moved often in the first three years as Louis took a succession of jobs with newspapers. About January, 1859, they came back to Mishawaka; then, a few months later, they went to Montgomery, Alabama, where the Barrett cousins with their printing connections helped Louis find work.

After a return to South Bend, probably alone, in the summer or fall of 1860, Emma gave birth to their daughter, Lottie, early in 1861. During the early months of the Civil War, she and Lottie rejoined her husband in Madison, Wisconsin, where his brother John also had located. Their son, Allie, was born in 1863.[3]

In the best of circumstances, the wife of a journeyman printer did not have an easy life. Typesetting, the printer's main task, was not highly paid, and usually involved night hours. Louis's drinking, as well as wartime inflation, put an additional economic burden on their lives, and Emma worked at various times during their marriage to increase their income. According to her later account, she tried dressmaking, millinery, working as an office "copyist," and taking in washing. (There was enough money, however, at least at times, to afford a hired girl.)[4]

She also continued to write, selling poems, stories and essays signed "Emma F. Pradt" to the *Mishawaka Enterprise, Montgomery Mail*, and *Wisconsin Patriot*, as well as the *North Iowa Times*. She tended to write a number of items on a similar subject, indicating that that subject was on her mind, and also that she had found a saleable theme.

Some of her pieces were lighthearted, but others vividly portrayed disillusionment with men who brought suffering to their wives and children, the worries of motherhood, and the death of girlhood dreams. In one poem she wrote, very dramatically,

> *Lost, lost, lost, a beautiful gladsome dream:*
> *Lost, forever lost, on Time's relentless stream...*
> *Ever, yes, ever thus, heart, must thou mourn –*
> *No glad to-morrow – no hope, now, for thee –*
> *Wrecked, ever wrecked, and lost, must thou be...*[5]

In another, she wrote of her mother's spirit coming to her like a comforting angel:

> *'Tis my mother's voice that's whispering low,*
> *Just as she did long, long years ago,*
> *Ere the grass had grown o'er her loving heart,*
> *And the death-angel riven our souls apart.*[6]

In Madison Emma found strong support in friendships, especially her friendship with Emile Cary, the wife of Lucius Cary, an employee of the *Wisconsin State Journal*. She returned to the Methodist church, after having been confirmed as an Episcopalian shortly after her marriage. And she occasionally enjoyed the relaxation of singing and playing her guitar in their house on Lake Street near Lake Mendota.[7]

But much greater sorrow was to come. In October, 1863, their two-year-old daughter Lottie died, and only ten months later, in August, 1864, their son Allie, one-and-a-half, died also. The tragedy of her children's deaths would never leave her.

In her writings, she expressed not only her own grief, but also compassion for her readers who had lost small children, or who had lost a loved one in the war. Each piece was a small sermon, ending in a declaration of faith.

> *"This cruel war" is not yet over; and to you, wives,*
> *mothers, sisters—all who have yielded your loved ones*
> *to your country, I write these words of hope and trust.*
> *Cast thy burden on the Lord, and he shall sustain thee.*[8]

In 1865, as the war ended and her "year of mourning" for Allie came to a close, Emma began to write frequently for the *Wisconsin Capitol.* Writing conventional pieces under her own name, some expressing nostalgia for her youth, she also began something very new: a series of satirical letters under the pseudonym "Polly Wiggins."

The character of "Polly Wiggins" was a thirty-eight-year-old, unmarried country woman, owning just one dress, who scandalized her neighbors by going to Madison to be near her fiance, "Josh." Using a misspelled English popular with humorists of the time (like "Josh Billings," "Petroleum V. Nasby," and Frances Whitcher's "Widow Bedott"), "Polly" satirized the foibles of both men and women, especially fashionable women:

> *The ladies here have got awful grate heads of hare, and*
> *they come them in a little lace bag, and then tie about*
> *ten yard of ribbin on it, and I cant think of anything*
> *else but our banty topnot chickens.*[9]

As a roving reporter, "Polly" poked fun at many aspects of Madison life: the theatre, a Methodist minister's severity, the antics of the state legislature. "Polly" also espoused women's rights. As a very homey example, soon after her wedding to "Josh," when her new husband forbade her to ice skate, she went out and skated anyway.

> *I frose mi feet, and mi nose, and mi eers, and made a hoal in my head, by the fall on the ise; and I barked mi arm, and lamed my back, but I'll lern tew skate if it kills me, just bekause Josh sed I shouldent...I am goin to show him that I beleave in women's rites, and I am goin tew live up tew it, tew.*[10]

The columns were a success. "Polly" won notice, even inspiring a bill in the legislature.[11]

But "Polly"'s career soon came to an end. In the last letter of the series in 1866, "Polly" suddenly became a fictional "vidder" (widow). For Emma herself, home for some time had been beckoning her back. Now, unwilling to continue her life with Louis Pradt any longer, Emma took the courageous step of leaving him and returning to South Bend.

4
A NEW LIFE
1867-1871

South Bend in 1867 was a bustling, growing city, rapidly indus-
trializing like most northern cities after the war and full of new opportunities. Emma Pradt found work teaching, and that summer filed
for divorce from her husband through an attorney, taking advantage
of Wisconsin's liberalized divorce laws, which allowed for grounds of
"habitual drunkenness."[1]

In her spare time, she sang and played her guitar at an occasional
amateur concert. And she wrote a few pieces, some under the pseudonyms "Mabel Clare" and "Anna Maria Stubbs," for the *St. Joseph Valley Register* and the *South Bend National Union*, successor to the old
Forum.[2]

Edward Molloy, the twenty-four-year-old editor of the *National
Union*, was struggling to bring his paper out of debt. Though of Irish
Catholic background, he had much in common with Emma. Both were
writers, both had been motherless children, both had known much
suffering (he having served three years in the 87th Indiana Infantry,
which participated in many battles), and both were strong temperance
advocates.

A later account characterized Edward as "a sober, industrious,
honest, sensible man of excellent habits and broad, generous views."
Born in New York, he had come west as a child to be brought up by a
family named Borden in nearby LaPorte County and had graduated
from the New Carlisle Collegiate Institute. After the war, he had come
to South Bend to take charge of the failing Democratic weekly.[3]

Edward and Emma developed a close friendship, and on Thanksgiving Day, 1867, just two weeks after her divorce from Louis was
granted, they were married by a Methodist clergyman.[4]

Now her two ambitions, for useful and fulfilling work and for a
happy domestic life, came together. As Mrs. Edward Molloy, Emma
also married the *National Union*. Their partnership gave her a new lease
on life. She thrived on the challenges presented by a less-than-successful
Democratic newspaper in a predominantly Republican town. She rev-

eled in the knowledge that she, a woman, could not only help her husband find solutions to the paper's problems, but also use it as a vehicle for her own ideas, and, she increasingly learned, as a ministry to her readers.[5]

To be able to work at all, she had to have help with the daily mountain of housework that faced her in their house near the *National Union* office, where they boarded three employees. Good servants were hard to come by. She advertised for

> . . . . *a professor-ess of the dish-rag persuasion...a girl with some idea of breadbaking, and who can cook a steak without someone standing beside her to turn it . . . . In fact most any kind of a girl who does not feel too much above her business to do a small share of the housework . . .*[6]

The girl she hired was one of a series of hired girls and foster daughters who would help free her for "outside" work throughout her life.

Moving to an apartment in the same building as the *National Union* office, on West Washington Street near Main, also must have helped. Among her prized possessions, she noted one day in the paper, were pictures she had hung on the wall of her baby Allie and of Emile Cary, her friend from Madison.[7]

Emma soon saw that the paper had two great problems: too few readers and subscribers, and lagging payments by both subscribers and advertisers. To attract more readers, she contributed many lively items of local news, and personalized the paper, balancing her husband's articles on political and economic matters with long, heartfelt obituaries, essays full of praise for local people, and anecdotes, stories and poems, both serious and humorous, drawn from her own memory and present life.

Having grown up in South Bend, the people she wrote about were often old friends. This fact, coupled with her own life experience, gave her words of sympathy or congratulations special power, both to actually help her neighbors—and to sell papers.

At the same time, Emma took over much of the paper's business management. While personally collecting overdue payments, she urged that the paper go on a cash-in-advance basis, which it did in January, 1869. She saved money, she later said, by learning the painstaking art of typesetting and occasionally running the press. For one year, during 1869, the Molloys used pre-printed inner pages called "patent insides," which greatly reduced the amount of writing and typesetting needed.[8]

In the next two years, the *National Union*, though never highly successful, got out of debt and held its own. One considerable help was an improving journalistic climate. At long last, professionalism was beginning to replace the old name-calling animosity between editors. The Molloys were active in the Northern Indiana Editorial Association, a new organization formed by the editors of the Tenth and Eleventh Congressional Districts. Friendships grew at the editors' semi-annual meetings, where they discussed common problems; and they communicated constantly through printed "exchanges." Quite often these "exchanges" were full of jokes and quips. The other editors found the editor-couple an interesting novelty.[9]

Emma's gregarious personality proved an advantage in her work. So did combining her vivid curiosity about people and their stories with some of her developing interests. This helped shape the paper's character, and also led her into activities that went beyond it.

Music, for example, was important to her, and when the well-known composer George F. Root came to town as head of a summer music school, the Normal Musical Institute, she gave coverage in the paper. Actually, she and Edward were among its organizers. And she wrote profiles of James G. Clark, a poet, songwriter and performer who gave concerts locally and became a lifelong friend.[10]

Another interest, one she shared with her father, was history. Emma served as secretary-librarian of the newly formed St. Joseph County Historical Society, collecting reminiscences, old newspapers, and old documents from longtime residents. She wrote historical sketches for the *National Union*, and began an ambitious "History of the St. Joseph Country," on which she would work for several years. It gave her a reason to indulge her zest for travel as she visited other northern Indiana towns to interview the older pioneers.[11]

Though hardly trouble-free, travel was much improved since Emma's youth, and increasingly was taking on the lure of adventure. Somehow she and her husband found time to go to New York in July, 1868, to attend a Democratic veterans' convention, where she read a long patriotic poem she had written.

Starting in 1869, they attended annual fall reunions of Edward Molloy's regiment, for which she also composed poetry. There were trips to visit her old friends in Madison, and many other excursions during their years in South Bend. Each trip resulted in at least one lively article for the *National Union*.[12]

The cause of the advancement of women had long been on her mind. Now she took an interest in the resurgent women's rights movement, often derided by the press for its "strong-minded women." She read the new journal, *Sorosis*, and also the *Revolution*, the woman suffrage paper published by Susan B. Anthony and Elizabeth Cady Stanton, whose office the Molloys visited briefly on their New York trip in 1868. The *National Union* began to feature reprinted editorials by Stanton, Anthony, and other female reformers.[13]

Echoing their radicalism, Emma wrote her own editorials arguing strongly for the vote for women and for greater opportunities in education and work. She urged young women to raise their sights above a protective home and a stifling social life, to educate themselves and enter the working world. To aid this effort, the Molloys hired female typesetters.[14]

Emma Molloy and her husband strongly condemned men who did not respect women's dignity, even street loafers with their insulting catcalls. She wrote even more passionately in favor of a woman's right to divorce an abusive husband.

On this then controversial issue, Emma supported the conduct of the actress Abby Sage McFarland Richardson, an acquaintance from her Madison days who had come to Indiana, then known as "the land of divorces," to divorce her husband, and who was now at the center of a national press scandal. As part of a long editorial, Emma wrote,

...the day is dawning when legal marital slavery must be abolished in America, when the laws will recognize

the right of a woman to free herself from a besotted husband as sacred as that of a man similarly situated.[15]

And when a local woman was condemned by a writer for having an abortion, Emma editorialized, as "Aunt Nabby,"

Crimes are sometimes committed against all the purer holier feelings of our nature under the cloak of marriage, and if woman, with the natural instinct of self-preservation, fly to this last resort–who ought to be educated to a better code of morals–the husband or wife?[16]

The Molloys also did not ignore temperance, another important women's issue. Emma was alarmed at the amount of drinking she witnessed among young men, and wrote about what it had done to a number of her former school classmates. Some of them, in fact, were dead.[17]

She began to participate in the women's movement in other ways. Using the satirical skills honed in her "Polly Wiggins Letters," she published provocative articles under pseudonyms in Stanton and Anthony's *Revolution* in 1869. In "A Chapter on Women," "Mrs. Pat Molloy" attacked prevailing prejudices in regard to women:

Wouldn't it be quite as sensible to say all men must be laborers or mechanics as it is to pass the edict that all women be housekeepers?...if God has created a woman with taste and brains for literature, art or science, then why, in the name of heaven, should she hide her talents in a napkin?[18]

She attended the Western Woman Suffrage Convention in Chicago that September, offering her comments about the need for women to take decisive steps out of the household "sphere," and proposing that men who abused alcohol or smoked were unfit to be fathers.[19]

One of the first barriers trail-blazing American women were breaking through was the custom that women should not appear before the public as speakers, or, as typically phrased at that time, "lecturers." In January, 1870, following the lead of pioneers such as Anna Dickinson and Mary Livermore, she presented her first public lecture, "Woman," at Good's Opera House in South Bend, and later in six nearby towns.

Her lectures stirred considerable interest. Though no texts have survived, newspaper accounts describe how she urged better education and health practices, and expansion of rights and opportunities for women.

The accounts showed approval of her smooth speaking style and her calm use of logic—not at all what was expected from the dreaded "strong-minded woman." The following year she spoke on "Marriage," defending Indiana's liberal divorce laws, just as Governor Conrad Baker was urging the Indiana General Assembly to tighten the state's residency requirements.[20]

One of Emma's major contributions to women's aspirations was her own example of hard work and success in a man's field. Other publications, including *Harper's Bazaar*, took note of her efforts. After she became pregnant late in 1869, that example became all the more conspicuous. In addition to lecturing and visiting Madison the next spring, she kept working far into the summer.[21]

In June, 1870, a group of visiting German Turners from Fort Wayne stopped in at the *National Union* office. They reported that Emma was "the only lady journalist in the State...an advocate of female suffrage...a spicy writer, a ready conversationalist, and has more energy and good judgment than some men we know of. She is a little less than medium size, blonde complexion, and is sapping health and constitution by her great mental exertions."[22]

For her part, with her now frequent use of humor, Emma wrote in the *National Union* of her struggle physically during hot summer weather:

> *Running a newspaper in the summer time is very much like a 250-lb. female going through 'Fat Man's Misery' in the Mammoth Cave—they got through it but can't tell how.*[23]

When Franklin (named for Benjamin Franklin, the hero of print-ers) was born in late August, 1870, the *National Union* reported that Emma was "son struck." She did not lie in bed long, but with the aid of her husband and other "baby tenders," was soon up and working again. In early November, the Molloys took Frank along on a two-week excursion by train and riverboat to the deep South, sponsored by the editors' association.[24]

It was, indeed, a new and highly invigorating life.

5
AN ITCH FOR CHANGE
1871-1873

Emma and Edward Molloy had found a second community of friends in the neighboring editors and their wives. In June, 1871, another editors' excursion, to Iowa and Nebraska, helped arouse Emma's interest in the West.[1]

She praised the northern Indiana editors highly for accepting her on the same terms as a man. They even helped publicize her lectures. Therefore she was shocked to discover, at a meeting of the Editors' and Publishers' Association of Indiana in Indianapolis, that as a woman she was barred from the editors' banquet.

> *We presented ourselves at the door of the banquet hall, to which as members of the Association we held tickets. The astute proprietor however had discovered that banqueting was "out of our sphere," and, with an elevation of his nasal organ...informed us "it was not intended for ladies."*[2]

She commiserated with her friend Laura Ream of Indianapolis, one of the few other female Hoosier journalists.

Less than complete acceptance by some of the people of South Bend may have been even more painful, one suspects when reading several pieces in the *National Union* which condemned gossip, or sympathetically defended a woman "disgraced" by divorce. About vicious gossips, she wrote, under the name "Belle Beach,"

> *Worse than the murderer, they seek to kill the soul, to crush the heart, to wither every good impulse, and destroy all trust in human nature.*[3]

There was, after all, so much about her that was different, so much that was daring, unconventional and even strange—her history, the roles she played as opinionated writer and speaker. Yet Emma had many friends in South Bend as well, whose attitude was surely full of admiration.

At any rate, with the paper not proving extremely profitable, the Molloys were becoming ready to try something new. After the unusually hot summer and early fall of 1871, including a trip to Chicago to report on the devastation caused by the Great Fire, the Molloys, believing they had made the *National Union* as successful as they could, took advantage of a chance to sell it.

After a Christmas night reception for their friends at South Bend's Dwight House, in January, 1872 they set off for Cortland, New York to take charge of the *Cortland Journal,* a Republican paper. Republican editors in northern Indiana praised them for changing their politics.[4]

However, this new transplantation of their lives did not last, possibly because of a lengthy illness of Emma's that spring, possibly for some other reason. The Molloys stayed in Cortland only briefly. Within a few months they had sold the *Journal* and were back in South Bend, discussing the idea of heading toward the West.[5]

Instead, they found a good opportunity just a few miles east, in the town of Elkhart. In August, 1872, not too long after Emma had recovered from her illness, the Molloys published the first issue of their new *Elkhart Observer.* In their opening editorial, they promised "fresh" and "reliable" local news. They also noted that their type had arrived just in time, but without any "t's." John F. Funk, the nearby editor of the Mennonite *Herald of Truth,* had saved the day by loaning them some.

The *Observer* was the second Republican paper in Elkhart, backed financially by a few men who disagreed with policies of the *Review.* Some predicted disaster for the new paper. But by offering lively, well-written coverage of local events, and items of interest to women, the *Observer* would win a large following.[6]

The Molloys already knew many Elkhart people from their earlier travels and historical research, and quickly made themselves at home. Their friends included Franklin Miles, then a medical student, later a physician and founder of the Dr. Miles Medical Company, and his wife, Ellen, with whom they intrepidly took a camping trip by boat down the St. Joseph River—fully written up by Emma Molloy in the *Observer.*[7]

Emma became prominent in the women's aid society, which gave help to poor families, and served as Worthy Matron of the Eastern Star. She contributed an occasional poem or musical selection on public occasions and continued work on her "History of the St. Joseph Country."

Their own household was a busy one. In addition to their little boy, Frank, now two years old, they adopted a little girl of six, "a soldier's orphan" named Mary Frances Pogue. They renamed her De'Etta Molloy and called her "Etta." A servant girl helped things go smoothly. Others also were in their household, at least at times.[8]

To help run the paper, the Molloys eventually found a third partner, Robert K. Brush, who also was Elkhart's postmaster. In August, 1873, they moved the *Observer* from the Brodrick's Opera House building on Main Street to the basement of the postoffice on West Jackson Boulevard. Another paper slyly referred to the *Observer* as a "triangular, subterranean concern."[9]

The *Observer* developed along much the same lines as the *National Union*. In addition to the standard political articles and market reports, it offered local and personal anecdotes, humorous exchanges with other editors, detailed travel letters, and historical sketches of the pioneers. Among their trips was one in November, 1872 to LaCygne, Kansas, to visit Emma's old friend Emile Cary, who had settled there.[10]

Emma also entertained, aided and instructed her female readers with a weekly column, "The Hearthstone," offering a steady stream of recipes, housekeeping tips, and parenting advice, often gleaned from correspondents or neighbors. For example,

> *I dropped in to see Mrs. DeCamp one day this week and found her making bread pudding of sour milk, and being assured that it was delicious I asked for the receipt. We have since tried it, and find it splendid: "Break your bread crumbs into one quart of sour milk...Add four eggs, a heaping teaspoonful of soda, one tablespoonful of corn-starch. Bake, and when ready to serve, make a boiled sauce of butter, sugar and flour...*[11]

Again, in her editorials, Emma spoke out on women's rights. She urged women to become more independent and to free themselves from abuse. She listed and highly praised the small but growing group of women who worked in local businesses. She published the writings of well-known feminists. And she encouraged her readers, male and female, to take the train to South Bend to attend inspirational lectures by Anna Dickinson, Mary Livermore and Abby Sage Richardson, and to hear Elizabeth Cady Stanton when she came to Elkhart.[12]

In an editorial on the value of female reformers, Emma wrote,

> *Commend us to the man who expresses his admiration for Susan Anthony behind her grim spectacles, marshaling the working women of New York, or Anna Dickinson, riding on an Iowa storm to deliver a lecture...*[13]

The popular speaker, writer and woman suffrage leader Mary Livermore was particularly admired by Emma. Emma called her "the greatest female orator in the United States." The two would become acquainted as fellow lecturers and reformers.[14]

As in South Bend, Emma Molloy had a strong voice in the management of the paper, and hired female help in the office. She became known as a tough businesswoman. The verve and confidence of her writings in the *Observer* indicate that she had found a satisfying and productive niche as a writer and editor in Elkhart, and a career that blended well with her life as a wife and mother. Influence, usefulness, service to others, enjoyment, all came together for the "editress." [15]

She felt pride in her success in managing both career and home. In a later address she said,

> *...Woman is particularly suited to the work of journalism, because of her natural ability to "keep several irons in the fire." I have known a woman to cast a roller while she was cooking her dinner...I believe the care of our households is very much overdone...My boy is just as happy and healthy for having been much of the time thrown upon his own resources...than if I had spent that precious three years' time*

in holding and rocking him, and dosing him with Godfrey's Cordial and Mrs. Winslow's Soothing Syrup.[16]

But there was a darker side to things. Her earlier losses continued to disturb her and played a part in her growing interest in spiritualism. Both Molloys suffered from illnesses. And in May, 1873, the *Elkhart Review* and *Elkhart Democratic Union* described her collapse one afternoon in the *Observer* office from "overwork," suffering a lengthy seizure of some kind, during which she hurt herself. Though such seizures had occurred before, the *Review* wrote, this was her worst attack so far.[17]

Finally, there was the nagging temperance question. Elkhart had grown quickly in the early 1870s, with the establishment of railroad repair shops and other industries. The temperance-minded editors of the *Observer* decried the fact that saloons were multiplying, and gambling and prostitution were increasing. Soon Emma would become deeply involved in fighting the evil of drink, and would leave her comfortable niche forever for the excitement and the uncertainties of a public life.

6
THE CRUSADER
1874-1875

In the spring and summer of 1874, in the cities, towns and villages of the Midwest, it was common to see a group of women in their long dresses and bonnets gathered on the sidewalk in front of a saloon, praying and singing hymns in an effort to influence the owner and his patrons to stop serving and drinking alcoholic beverages. Emma Molloy would become one of these temperance crusaders, and more.

As she worked with her husband at the *Observer* office, or walked along the wooden sidewalks past the saloons with their odors of liquor, their doorway loungers who included small boys, Emma, still full of memories of her first husband's alcoholism, and now the mother of a three-year-old boy, felt much anger.

She was not alone. Throughout America, people were becoming increasingly alarmed at the ills of alcohol use and abuse. To many, limitation or prohibition of the liquor trade seemed crucial for the well-being of society.

Middle-class women were especially drawn to this belief, because so many saw alcohol's serious ill effects in their own families and communities. And men's freedom to spend time and money in saloons symbolized their wider freedoms—to vote, to be actors on the political and economic stage. Emma Molloy would describe the women's temperance movement of the 1870s as

> . . . *a natural revulsion, an eruption of the smouldering fires that have for centuries past been pent up in the heart of woman.*[1]

Throughout the country as they worked together, thousands of women would gain courage to speak, write, and act as never before. Emma Molloy at thirty-four, already a skilled writer and an enthusiastic, effective public speaker, a women's rights advocate, and with considerable experience in organizations, was well fitted and eager to play a part in the movement.

Temperance movements were not new. Well before the Civil War, restrictive laws had been passed in several states, most notably in Maine. Indiana's own restrictive laws had long ago been overturned; but in 1873 a resurgence of temperance activity produced the controversial Baxter Law, authored by William Baxter, a Quaker of Richmond. This very strict law required a majority of a ward's voters to sign every petition for a liquor license, and specified certain criminal offenses. During 1873 Emma worked with other local temperance people for its enforcement.[2]

Then early in 1874 news came of the mighty Woman's Crusade, which had succeeded in closing saloons in Ohio and was spreading throughout the Midwest. It would lead shortly to the formation of the National Woman's Christian Temperance Union. Emma, in her editorial on March 4, expressed much admiration for the Crusade when she wrote,

> *It has convinced the world that womankind are terribly in earnest; that the idea of their contentment is an erroneous one...God bless this noble sisterhood...*[3]

When a crowd of Elkhart women met later that month to begin an Elkhart Crusade, she was among the organizers.[4]

However, from the start, she saw wider opportunities. In fact, her first Crusade speech was given in her native city of South Bend on March 15, 1874, sharing the speakers' platform with now ex-Vice President Schuyler Colfax whom she had known since childhood. Within a few weeks, cramming her schedule full, she had spoken at Goshen, La Porte, Plymouth, Kentland, Valparaiso, Niles, Michigan, and Harvard, Illinois, as well as in Elkhart. By July she had spoken also in Ohio and Wisconsin.[5]

Emma Molloy turned out to be a simply spellbinding temperance speaker. Two years later, Frances E. Willard, the great temperance reformer, soon to lead the National WCTU, would characterize her as "a much better speaker than any woman now before the public as a temperance lecturer."[6]

Emma wooed her audiences with a mixture of argument, sarcasm, dramatic pathos, humor, and uplifting inspiration. In the most graphic language, she dramatized the damage done by liquor to her family and friends. She attacked the liquor industry with strong metaphors of murder, damnation, fire, war, revolution:

> *The two armies meet and the world looks on while woman enters places which before have echoed only to the tread of man.*[7]

And she challenged the Crusaders to go beyond their universal tactic of pressuring men for moral reform, to think and work in political ways.[8]

Crusaders in Elkhart, as in many places in Indiana, were active on both fronts. Delegations of women went to saloon owners and asked for a pledge to stop selling liquor. When they were rebuffed, as often happened, they staged a massive sidewalk protest. Groups of praying, singing women gathered daily at the "rumseller's," sometimes confronting angry crowds. The women also persuaded many individual men to sign temperance pledges.[9]

It was an effort appreciated by many in the community. In the midst of the Elkhart Crusade, one poor woman urged the Crusaders to persevere in their work with these words: "I wash six days in the week and iron six nights, to support these men, and half my earnings, at least, my husband spends at Shumard & Golden's Saloon."[10]

At inspirational meetings, one Elkhart woman after another tried public speaking for the first time. Well over two hundred women, including wives of some of Elkhart's most prominent men, took part in the drive that temporarily succeeded in closing a number of saloons.

But some of the women did more. Under the leadership of Emma Molloy and others, they worked with leading temperance men to successfully elect a "temperance" ticket to town offices in May, 1874. They participated in legal battles, which often were less successful, against liquor dealers who did not comply with the law. A Pinkerton's detective was hired to help convict one offender.[11]

In turn, the Molloys and other leading Crusaders and temperance men were sued for damages. Finally, knowing that the Baxter Law might be repealed, city and county organizations of Crusaders were formed to try to influence the upcoming elections and party platforms.[12]

Lecturing throughout the state that summer and fall, Emma worked to strengthen a statewide movement for the enforcement and retention of the Baxter Law. Everywhere she went, she met active groups of women Crusaders and the men who aided them.

At Delphi, for example, Emma spoke to a large audience at the courthouse, and the next day made sure to visit the offices of both the *Times* and the *Journal*. In one of her series of "On the Road" articles in the *Observer*, she profiled the town and its residents. She marveled that an Episcopal priest, the Rev. Stimpson, had given temperance sermons at all the schools in the county. And she noted,

> *The great clog upon the wheels of Temperance here is a pros-*
> *ecuting attorney who is in constant consultation with the*
> *'rummies.' They have a lawyer, however, Mr. Joseph Sims,*
> *who is a very active worker in the temperance cause. He*
> *donates his time and talents to the good work. God bless such*
> *men.*[13]

She ran into opposition that summer, very close to home, when she attempted to speak at a Grange picnic in Goshen. Charles L. Murray, editor of the *Goshen Democrat*, not a supporter of the Crusade, or of Emma Molloy, reported that they refused to hear Emma's "stereotyped, crusading temperance harangue." She was "unmistakably snubbed ...they would not hear her any way it could be shaped." The *Observer*, however, pointed to the influence of a certain inebriated member in keeping Emma from speaking.[14]

In early September, when the Indiana Woman's Christian Temperance Union was organized in Indianapolis by temperance people of both sexes, Emma was there. She gave a report on Elkhart County's activities, and served on a committee which wrote a strong resolution pledging the Indiana WCTU to work for retention of the Baxter Law.[15]

Though opponents of the law won a majority in the Indiana General Assembly, she and others circulated a petition in some forty-seven counties, calling not only for retention of the law, but also for the addition of women's signatures to the required liquor license petitions.

On January 21, 1875, a large group of Indiana WCTU members attended a joint session of the General Assembly. They brought their petitions signed by 21,000 women. Zerelda Wallace, first president of Indiana's WCTU, gave an impassioned address.[16]

But as expected, the General Assembly soon replaced the law with a weaker statute. Not long afterward, Emma declared to a group of woman suffrage advocates that in reaching the peak of their influence in Indiana and other states,

> *Through the stern lessons of those days, woman learned how puny was the hand that held no ballot.*[17]

7
Beyond the Crusade
1875-1878

Believing fervently in woman suffrage, Emma Molloy raised the issue in most of her early speeches, opening her to special criticism from some of her fellow editors. In the Indiana WCTU itself, many who were not ready to engage in political work found Emma's approach, including her advocacy of woman suffrage, too radical—despite the personal sentiments of president Zerelda Wallace, who had been "converted" by her negative experience with the Indiana General Assembly. Emma's address at the 1875 Indiana WCTU state convention, in which she said prayer was ineffective in fighting alcohol, gave particular offense to many of the women.[1]

Throughout her temperance career, even when the National WCTU widened its efforts politically under the leadership of Frances Willard, Emma would depend upon and work with and for the WCTU, but never confine herself within it. She was an independent personality—and as in her editorial experiences, she often found working with men more productive and satisfying. Furthermore, she always envisioned coalitions of people, male and female, moving toward a common goal.[2]

During her travels in 1874, she had been inspired by the oratory and personal example of Jerome J. Talbott, a reformed alcoholic and leader of the Indiana branch of the Independent Order of Good Templars. He became a close friend.

For some years Emma had belonged to this popular fraternal order of abstainers, which accepted both men and women. In August, 1874, she and Talbott had both attended and spoken before a huge rally at Tippecanoe, attended by Good Templars from all over the state.[3]

Now, in the wake of the Baxter Law's defeat and her rejection as "too radical" by the Indiana WCTU, she went to work for the Good Templars, organizing over twenty chapters throughout Indiana. In 1875 she and Talbott also joined in publishing a monthly journal, the *Advance Guard,* aimed at temperance people throughout the state.[4]

She no longer seems to have spent much time at the *Observer* office—though she continued to write for it, sending letters from her lecture tours, as well as writing for the *Chicago Inter-Ocean* and other Chicago papers.[5]

She was, in fact, finding a new life's mission in her temperance work. She later wrote that, having suffered from the results of alcoholism, she felt impelled to enter the fight against liquor

> ...*as a fireman rushes into a burning building with no thought for himself, but with one inspiration, to save the perishing.*[6]

As years went on, her commitment to this "rescuing" deepened.

Yet these words, like the explanations of many successful "career women" of her era, were only partly true. She thrived on the challenges of this new calling, the travel, the excitement, the widening friendships, the chances to meet and become acquainted with inspiring leaders. Perhaps most of all, Emma fully appreciated the power to move people she had discovered in herself as a lecturer. She put herself forward aggressively, and managed the progress of her career in a well organized, businesslike fashion, as she had learned to do as a newspaper publisher, making skillful use of both the platform and the press.[7]

Increasingly, she chose to pursue her new career even at the cost of happiness in her home life. Her absences from Edward, their small son Frank, and their daughter Etta grew longer and longer—though occasionally Frank did travel with his mother. Edward, while very supportive of her efforts, eventually began to suffer from her lack of attention. She also risked criticism and suspicion in an era when women were just beginning to break out of the domestic mold, by working so often in partnership with men.[8]

Her career rapidly broadened. In October, 1874, while still in the midst of her Indiana work, she gave a long, stirring speech on "Country Journalism" at the second Woman's Congress in Chicago. Attending were some of America's foremost women. The next year she was a delegate to the International Temperance Conference in Chicago. And representing the Woman Suffrage Association of Indiana, of which she was elected a vice president, she spoke at the American Woman Suffrage Association's convention in New York in November, 1875.

Articles by and about her began to appear in the *Woman's Journal,* the leading woman suffrage weekly published in Boston by Lucy Stone. Throughout her career, she often wrote her own press releases.[9]

In 1876 she lectured in Massachusetts for several weeks on behalf of the Massachusetts Temperance Alliance, the state's Prohibitionist Party, the Good Templars, and other organizations. She joined James Redpath's roster of "lyceum" speakers. She attended and spoke at the New England Woman Suffrage Association's annual meeting in Boston. That summer, she was a delegate to the International Temperance Conference at Philadelphia and toured the Centennial Exposition, writing her views of both in the *Woman's Journal.*[10]

Her times at home also were busy that year. The Molloys sold the *Observer* and decided to move back to South Bend, to a house on West Washington Street. Edward Molloy would hold a variety of jobs, including selling insurance, before becoming editor of the *LaPorte Chronicle* in 1878.[11]

Joining the Ribbon workers now brought an undreamed-of expansion and a greater depth to Emma's lecturing career. Over and over again, in her first marriage to Louis Pradt, she had tried to "rescue" him from alcohol, and had failed. Now she found something that opened a channel for her to minister directly to alcoholics. It was a new approach for her, one that combined temperance and religion.[12]

The Ribbon movement, a mass phenomenon of the 1870s, blended aspects of a revival with a mutual-support psychology. It was in some ways a forerunner of the Alcoholics Anonymous movement that began some sixty years later. At a series of meetings, led by a stirring speaker like the reformed alcoholic Francis Murphy, or Emma Molloy herself, often dozens or even hundreds of men would be persuaded to "take the pledge" and pin the symbolic ribbon of reform to their lapels.

A club of pledged men then formed which met frequently for support. At each meeting, certain members shared their life stories. Emma affectionately referred to the members of her Ribbon clubs as "my boys." In small towns, her efforts tended to stir up the entire community.

Typically, without a strong program, Ribbon pledges were broken, and the clubs formed by the men fell apart. But Emma Molloy's work sometimes had special impact. Unlike some temperance speakers, she stepped down from the platform and worked with individuals, often going to great lengths to counsel and persuade them, then following through with referrals to hospitals and other personal efforts.

Hospitals she favored included the Boston Washingtonian Home, headed by Dr. Albert Day. This institution was in the vanguard in treating alcoholism as a disease rather than simply a problem of personal morality.[13]

Emma began her Ribbon work while lecturing in Massachusetts in 1876 and had considerable success. Her spiritual commitment to the Ribbon cause was deepened when Jerome J. Talbott, her close Good Templar friend and mentor, died at the Molloys' home in South Bend after relapsing into drinking. In his dying days he pledged to be with her in spirit as she, in effect, carried on his efforts.[14]

Emma continued her Ribbon work in Vermont early in 1877. Despite encountering a great deal of resistance, and becoming seriously ill at one point, she pledged at least 2,000 members into Ribbon clubs.

During her travels that winter and spring she took side trips, and composed long letters for the *Indianapolis Journal* full of her observations of New England. One described Boston's working women; another, an evening she spent with the poet John Greenleaf Whittier in his home in Amesbury, Massachusetts.[15]

That spring also she came back to South Bend and, aided by her husband, founded a Ribbon organization called the South Bend Reform Club. It was a noteworthy event, fully described in local newspapers and even in a local history. The community became very much involved. The *South Bend Tribune* remarked, "Red ribbons grow in favor day by day...the young man who doesn't wear one is the exception." And it noted also that, unlike some earlier temperance movements, "This awakening has taken hold of the class who have been in the most urgent need of help." At one meeting, Emma spoke out against use of tobacco as well.[16]

In May she took time out from her Ribbon work to attend the national convention of the Good Templars in Portland, Maine. The organization had split the year before over the admission of African-Americans. Favoring their admission, she worked for a change in the rules which might improve their status within the remaining organization, but the effort failed.

At that meeting, as a Good Templar officer, she also composed a telegram to the First Lady, Mrs. Rutherford B. Hayes, asking if wine were to be kept off the White House menu for public receptions.[17]

Early in 1878 she went again to Massachusetts to conduct a grueling Ribbon campaign, fully five months long, that brought in a reported total of over 100,000 temperance pledges. She also appeared before a legislative committee at the Massachusetts State House with state WCTU officials. She addressed the New England Woman Suffrage Association. And she was a delegate to the international convention of the breakaway segment of the Good Templars, the Right Worthy Grand Lodge of the World, in Boston.[18]

Two "testimonial receptions" were held in Boston that year in her honor, the first in late May, the second in early September on the eve of her departure for a much-anticipated trip to England. The great reformer Wendell Phillips was among those signing the invitation to the first reception.

At both events Dr. Albert Day of the Boston Washingtonian Home was a featured speaker. At the second, addresses were given by Emma's idol and now acquaintance, Mary Livermore, by an African-American Good Templars leader, Dr. William Wells Brown, and by several others prominent in New England temperance work. Mary Livermore expressed high hopes for Emma's mission to England, and spoke of the many mothers who had told her of their gratitude for Emma Molloy's work with their "boys."[19]

This was without any doubt a peak time in Emma Molloy's career. She was becoming well known. Her biography appeared in Phebe Hanaford's *Women of the Century,* and *The Ribbon Workers* by James Hiatt. Though she did not have as much time for woman suffrage efforts, the National Woman Suffrage Association listed her as one of its corresponding secretaries.[20]

The Ribbon Workers, typical of such biographical anthologies of the time, was flowery and gushing. The section devoted to Emma

Molloy was no exception. Along with several enthusiastic testimonials drawn from her Ribbon work, it gave a somewhat distorted version of her life. Her childhood was all misery; her first marriage all hardship (and ending in widowhood, not divorce); her discovery of her oratorical powers sudden and unexpected; her lectures and other services demanded, not offered.

This account gives us a good idea of how Emma, having always had a flair for the dramatic, was presenting her story in order to sway—and help—her listeners.

8

ENGLAND AND AFTERWARD
1878-1881

One of Emma's greatest triumphs and challenges was her lecturing trip to England in the fall of 1878. A primary stated purpose was to aid the growth of the budding Ribbon movement in England, and in a concentrated effort she did form a Ribbon club of several hundred members in one of London's poorest districts.

Much of her time, however, was devoted to speaking before the Good Templars and other temperance organizations and writing in their journals, describing the American crusades, advocating prohibition laws and woman suffrage, and blasting the polite custom of social drinking.[1]

London street life shocked her, and she found the middle and upper classes, especially women, and the established church far too complacent. Using some of her strongest rhetoric, she often described temperance as a war which women like herself, who had been severely scarred by alcoholism, had banded together to fight. She told one audience of the "revolution" which

> ...has shaken us, in America...from centre to circumference, and we have stripped from around the drink traffic the masks of sociability and respectability, and today it stands out in all its hideous deformity with the finger of scorn of every Christian woman in the country pointed out against it.[2]

From September to December she lectured daily, to audiences ranging from small, intimate gatherings to mass meetings of thousands, in various parts of London and in smaller towns such as Stratford, Shaftesbury, Boston, Weymouth, Enfield, Market Rasen, Dunstable, Hull, Preston, Lancaster, and others.

Armed with glowing letters of recommendation from her American friends, she soon became acquainted with leaders of England's temperance organizations, such as Margaret Lucas, sister of John Bright and president of the British Woman's Temperance Association; William Noble, whose meetings at Hoxton Hall, London, had begun the Ribbon movement in England; Joseph Malins, head of the breakaway segment of the Good Templars Emma favored; the Quaker missionaries to the East End of London, John and Marie Hilton; and the temperance workers Henry and Elizabeth Browne.

Some of her addresses in England were not confined to the temperance issue. At Victoria Park Tabernacle in London, she spoke to an audience of children, and their parents, on "Reaping the Whirlwind."

> *When you are tempted to dishonesty in however small a thing, remember, what we sow we must reap...When your lips begin to say a harmful thing of a neighbor, remember the words we speak cannot be recalled...they are like thistle-seeds, and may bring us and our friend a fearful harvest. When the wine cup tempts you, remember it is like sowing tares in the wheat field...Above all when tempted to go in bad company remember these words of a wise man, "It's safer to ride in a waggon whose lynch pins are loose than keep company with one whose morals are loose."* [3]

Emma's travels in England came to an end all too soon. One day in December she was returning from Yorkshire to London, and while changing trains at Wakefield, fell and seriously injured her back. Her new English friends took care of her with much solicitude, but she and the physicians decided she should return to America. She cancelled many planned engagements, including a tour of Scotland. Regretting her leaving, the *Good Templars' Watchword* engraved copies of her portrait for sale to its readers. [4]

Once she was home, however, before very long Emma had recuperated and was ready to work again. In the winter and spring of 1879, she gave lectures on her London experiences in South Bend and Mishawaka, in Rhode Island and Massachusetts. A few months later, she lectured for the WCTU in Massachusetts, where women had won the right to vote in school elections. Her appearances in several towns helped encourage women to register. [5] Also on her return, the *Temper-*

ance Cause, journal of the Massachusetts Total Abstinence Society, reported that Emma Molloy was writing up her London experiences for the *Morning and Day of Reform,* a monthly temperance journal published by Henry Waldo Adams of New York, and that she had accepted its associate editorship.

The paper was received and read by temperance people all over America. Leaders such as National WCTU president Frances Willard were readers and frequent contributors. Emma was now in a superb position to achieve influence through her writing skills.[6]

On a more personal note, she took some time out that summer of 1879 to help organize and attend a once-in-a-lifetime Barrett family reunion at Conesus Lake, New York. According to her own account, nearly 150 family members were there, including her father, William Barrett, and seven of his sisters and brothers, the oldest of whom was eighty-two. Many cousins were there, too, including one of her favorites, Morris Barrett, formerly of Montgomery, now a printer with the U. S. Government Printing Office in Washington.[7]

That summer, too, neighbors and members of the Reform Club in South Bend organized an impromptu fortieth birthday celebration for her at the Molloys' home on Washington Street. A cornet band furnished lively music. She seems for the next two or three years to have tried to make her absences from home a little less long and less far, though there would be very many. Her family life had become very stressful, however, as would become evident.[8]

As she returned to her temperance work in America and saw the limitations of the work she and others had been doing, she tried to focus her energies on what seemed the most effective and permanent reforms.

In her work with individuals, she had come to believe even more strongly that religious belief, in some cases a conversion, was necessary to make a temperance pledge last. She began to conduct temperance revivals in which she took the role of evangelist. As years went on, she sometimes had an assistant, and her campaigns could stretch out into several weeks, beginning with temperance and going on to obtain conversions.[9]

In fact, in the years 1879 to 1881, though very few denominations yet ordained women, she began occasionally appearing in a church pulpit—for example, at Methodist church services during the 1879 and 1880 conventions of the Indiana WCTU.[10]

One group of people she believed needed her help were the inmates at the Northern Indiana State Prison at Michigan City, many of whom had been affected by alcohol. Earlier, in the 1870s, she had begun to take an interest in the prison. After the Molloys moved to LaPorte in the spring of 1880, the prison was much closer. Now, when she was home, she often visited it, conducting an occasional Sunday service, counseling inmates and their families, and taking reading material to the prisoners. As her experience grew, she was appointed to the prison committee of the National WCTU.[11]

She also was concerned about the lives of the men after their release from prison. In her travels she had seen progressive efforts to rehabilitate ex-prisoners, such as Michael Dunn's House of Industry in New York. In 1880 she worked with other concerned people in Indiana, including WCTU members and Quaker prison reformer Charles F. Coffin, in holding meetings in Indianapolis to organize an Ex-Convicts' Aid Society, whose goal was to establish two halfway houses for released prisoners, one in northern, one in southern Indiana.[12]

But this aim was not pursued to completion, very likely because Emma, like many others, was turning her primary attention toward another great cause: the prohibition amendment battle.

Surveying the American scene, seeing the sale and consumption of alcohol not only not decreasing, but greatly increasing, and knowing the fragility of many temperance pledges, Emma and others had hardened their views on the necessity of prohibition laws. In 1879 she told a meeting of the Indianapolis WCTU,

> *This evil thing will not die of itself, therefore nothing remains as the hope of those of us who have suffered from its curse—not reform, not mitigation, but extirpation by means of prohibition. To rely wholly on moral suasion is simply idiotic.*[13]

She threw herself into a new effort, mounted by the usually scattered temperance forces, to obtain prohibition amendments to state constitutions. Kansas ratified the first such amendment in November, 1880, after an effort led by its teetotaling governor, John P. St. John.

Emma was among those who joined the speakers in Kansas that fall. She returned to Topeka in early 1881, addressing members of the Kansas legislature on behalf of strict prohibition laws, promoting woman suffrage, and earning the friendship of Governor St. John.[14]

In Indiana a Grand Temperance Council was formed in 1879 to work for a constitutional amendment. Headed partly by some of Emma's friends who had come to prominence in the Ribbon movement and the WCTU, it combined various temperance organizations into county committees throughout the state.

Partly through its own efforts, partly because the opposition was not well organized, the Grand Temperance Council succeeded in obtaining preliminary passage of a prohibition amendment by the Indiana General Assembly in 1881. But despite much effort, the amendment's chances were squelched in the 1883 session.[15]

For four years Emma was heavily involved in the fight, lecturing around the state, serving as state organizer for the Indiana WCTU, gathering petition signatures, and writing and editing for the *Morning and Day of Reform* (whose office Henry Waldo Adams, the editor, brought to LaPorte in 1881).

In her writing she battled frequently with the *Journal of Freedom and Right*, a pro-liquor paper of Indianapolis edited by Paul Schuster. In one editorial Emma produced figures to show how the liquor trade thrived among foreign immigrants. And she produced a biting, satirical two-page leaflet entitled *Liquor Dealers' Gospel No. 2*.

As usual, her work was intensive. From January to May, 1880, she lectured daily for ninety-eight days. She helped the Grand Temperance Council organize rallies for the amendment. For one meeting in LaPorte in the late summer of 1881, she brought in four top national figures: Frances Willard, John P. St. John, Neal Dow of Maine, and Sojourner Truth. She also espoused the woman suffrage amendment which received preliminary passage in 1881 and, like the other amendment, was later soundly defeated.[16]

Emma's status within the Indiana WCTU had grown considerably since the early days. At its annual meeting in 1881, she even received a few votes for president. It was partly a matter of all the time she had spent in organizational work. But it was also that at least some in the state organization now endorsed a change in the National WCTU's position on woman suffrage.

The National WCTU officially adopted woman suffrage as its cause at its convention in Washington in October, 1881. Some delegates, including Auretta Hoyt of Indianapolis, secretary of the Grand Temperance Council of Indiana, still did not agree, and formed a new organization.

As a delegate and reporter, Emma wrote a lively account of the convention for the *Morning and Day of Reform.* For a few minutes she herself rose to read to the convention and president Frances Willard a letter of encouragement from her friend, John P. St. John. This was a most gratifying moment.[17]

9
A TIME OF TRIAL
1882-1887

But for all Emma's success, there was a price to be paid. Her domestic life had deteriorated very badly —so much so that in the spring of 1882 she filed for divorce from Edward. Her complaint in the divorce suit was that at the time of her trip to England, Edward had brought his father and stepmother to live in their home. This was much against Emma's wishes, since his stepmother had long disapproved of her way of life, especially her friendships with temperance men.

After two years of discord, during which Edward's stepmother had accused her of "unchastity," he had agreed to ask the couple to move out; but in February, 1882, they returned. Emma refused to live with her husband after that. And she claimed that the older couple's presence was harmful as well to their son Frank, now eleven years old. The divorce was granted, on grounds of "cruelty," in April, 1882. One wonders if it was more a case of their lives, their worlds, growing irreparably far apart.[1]

Now began Emma's great time of trial. Without her home, her husband's support, her cloak of married respectability, she clung more tightly than ever to her ministry and reform work. Now in her forties, her figure grown matronly, she would travel west, encountering difficult conditions, suffering from illnesses and exhaustion, but not letting these things defeat her.[2]

Now more and more her home seems in a way to have been the pulpit and the lecture platform, and her neighbors all the new friends she made as a result, in whatever state and city they might be. For some time, her efforts to make an actual home were less successful.

In leaving Indiana she did take family with her, including Frank, of whom she had won custody; her daughter Etta; and three foster daughters, Cora, Ida, and Emma Lee. They moved from LaPorte to the city of Elgin, Illinois later in 1882, after the *Morning and Day of Reform* was purchased by the D. C. Cook Christian publishing house of Elgin. Some of the young people joined her in working for the paper.

For the job of business manager of the *Morning*, Emma suggested a younger friend, George A. Graham. This was to prove a tragic error. Graham was a convicted criminal, an ex-inmate of the Michigan City prison whom she had helped. From their home in Fort Wayne, at Emma's urging, George Graham brought his wife Sarah (from whom, however, he later claimed to be divorced) and their two young sons.[3]

With her family and the Grahams situated in Elgin, Emma continued to travel from time to time to give temperance speeches and revivals, handling some of her editorial work by correspondence. Completing her work in Indiana, she also spoke in Kansas. She strongly reproved the people of Leavenworth, where the new state prohibition laws were constantly being violated:

> *...in Leavenworth 108 saloons rule this city...there are hundreds of homes being destroyed and no outcry about it. Not a stone's throw from the house where I am stopping a man lay drunk on his porch the live long night. The wife was driven to insanity. The children are running wild . . .. Do you know where your criminals are coming from?*[4]

It may have been at this time also that she addressed and counseled with inmates at a nearby prison.[5]

In the fall of 1883, she went to Ohio for several weeks to give 155 speeches for the Ohio WCTU in its unsuccessful drive for a prohibition amendment, wearing herself to exhaustion and illness.[6] And that December she traveled to Oklahoma to give a series of temperance and Christian revival meetings to the Cherokee Indians at Tahlequah. Much was written of their success, of the hundreds who signed pledges and professed conversions, though she expressed her doubts in a poem in the *Cherokee Advocate:*

> *...Will your pledges still be honored?*
> *Will your ribbons still be wore*
> *Will temptation be resisted*
> *When this woman loved and honored*
> *Shall go hence and come no more?...*[7]

On her return from Elgin to Tahlequah for more work in January, 1884, ice in the Arkansas River blocked the ferry, and Emma and other travelers had to make their way across the river on the ice. Taking a mail hack to Tahlequah, she arrived at the reservation, noted the *Cherokee Advocate,* "cold and fatigued, but with zeal unabated."

She had been invited to stay for the winter, and did establish a home base at Tahlequah, bringing Frank and her foster daughter Cora Lee with her. But before long she herself was off to the small town of Washington, Kansas, where she held a very successful two-month temperance campaign and revival. She made many converts and friends.[8]

It is not surprising that in this period there were negative reactions to her, especially from some of the press who not only opposed her views on alcohol, but looked for opportunities to discredit reformers—in this case a female reformer who had left her husband.

A typical sentiment toward temperance reformers was expressed by the *Western Brewer,* a brewers' trade journal: "In America a vigorous crusade is being made to bring the brewers and their business into contempt. The people engaged in this work...are, first, the sectarians; second, the hypocrites of society; third, the uneasy and undomestic women, who think they were born with a 'mission.'"[9]

In June, 1882, in Wabash, Indiana, a fellow temperance worker had told the *Wabash Courier* about his infatuation with Emma. Other newspapers picked up the story. She had reacted swiftly, insisting on a public "investigation." When no misconduct whatsoever on her part was found, she was accused of using the publicity to attract larger crowds. Other articles pointed to a diamond ring and a gold watch chain as evidence that she was growing wealthy in her work.[10]

There was more controversy in 1884, when she moved her family and the Grahams to Washington, Kansas. In the late spring of that year, having returned from Washington to Tahlequah for more meetings with the Cherokees, she learned that the *Morning and Day of Reform* was for sale.

In a move she later described as less than wise, Emma decided to buy the journal, and in June, 1884, she, her son Frank, her daughter Etta, her foster daughters, George and Sarah Graham and their two sons all moved to Washington to live in a modest house built by her new friends. The journal was published in an office opposite the county courthouse.[11]

She needed a community and friends. Washington represented a new start. But it was a microcosm of the state. Kansas Republicans had not all supported Prohibition or now ex Governor St. John, nor had Democrats. With her writings and speeches she had already offended many in Kansas, including some in Washington. Now she used the *Morning* to support St. John's candidacy for President on the Prohibitionist ticket. This sealed her fate with Republicans.

Though she was by no means alone in her views—the national leadership of the WCTU, finding little support for prohibition in the two major parties, helped lead the Prohibitionist Party's campaign that year—her paper lost subscribers rapidly. Conducting lengthy revivals in neighboring towns, Emma poured the proceeds into the failing paper. But in the spring of 1885, it ceased publication. Emma turned over its list of subscribers to the *Voice,* a temperance paper of New York.

The *Western Brewer* gave its opinion of the situation of many of St. John's supporters: "The St. Johnites stand alone, accused of all mankind, stranded high and dry...This semi-crazy band of hypocrites has not now a spot on earth...It has lost its press."[12]

Graham's wife and children returned to Fort Wayne. But Emma gave a successful revival in Springfield, Missouri, where she was befriended by a wealthy temperance advocate, Judge James Baker, and his wife. She accepted Baker's offer to resettle with her family on a farm in nearby Brookline, and to pay Baker for it in installments.

George Graham came to Springfield, too, without family or occupation, on the understanding that he would manage the farm during her long absences. Now claiming to be divorced from his wife Sarah, he married Cora Lee, Emma's foster daughter, in July, 1885.[13]

Even greater problems were now to come. Gossip about the Molloy and Graham families had circulated for some time in the town of Washington, especially among enemies, and as soon as they had moved to Springfield, the *Washington Post* exploded with an "exposé" that claimed Emma and Graham had shared a hotel room in Kansas City.

Ignoring this threat to her reputation, Emma left Springfield for five solid months' revival work in Kansas towns. But she became increasingly uneasy at a strange report from Springfield: that Graham had brought back his two boys from Fort Wayne, and that Sarah Graham had come, too, as far as St. Louis, where she had "disappeared" at the railroad depot.

Sarah Graham's worried Indiana relatives and Springfield officials began to investigate. First they uncovered Graham's bigamy, and he was arrested and jailed. The *Fort Wayne News* and *Washington Post*, among others, blatantly accused him of murder. Then, in late February, 1886, while Emma was speaking in Illinois, a woman's body surrounded by Sarah Graham's clothing was found on the Molloy farm. Authorities charged Graham with murder. Emma and Cora Lee Graham were arrested as alleged accomplices.

Several weeks of sensation in the press followed. Reporters from far and wide went to Springfield to cover the case, especially relished by those papers supporting the liquor industry. Enemies in Washington also helped fuel the fire.

Graham, whose literary "bent" was aided by newspaper reporters, and who feared lynching, produced a bewildering stream of writings from his jail cell. He confessed to the murder; and he detailed supposed intimacies between himself and Emma, going back to the days they lived in Elgin, and Emma's supposed confessions of earlier sins.

Hundreds vied for a seat in the courtroom as many witnesses testified, including Graham's thirteen-year-old son Charlie, who also implied many intimacies between Emma and his father. Much pro and con was written about her, and she became, briefly, a famous example of the reformer held up to scorn.

A new and distorted picture of her emerged, as a hardened, cynical person, one who used others and tolerated, even encouraged or participated in, immorality. The *Fort Wayne Gazette* called her "The Viper at the Fireside," exhuming the Wabash incident.

Knowing her better, the *St. Joseph Valley Register* in South Bend believed her innocent of any knowledge of the murder, but called her a poor judge of character, too ready to accept unworthy people into her life.[14]

It is worth noting that Edward Molloy, at the helm of the *LaPorte Herald-Chronicle*, did not go along with his fellow journalists in printing story after story about his former wife.

The proceedings dragged on. In April, just as the *Springfield Herald* was about to release an illustrated tabloid-style book about the case, a mob lynched George Graham. A chapter on the lynching was added. The book, *The Graham Tragedy and the Molloy-Lee Examination*, packed full of Graham's writings, court testimony, and other sensational items, would pursue Emma for years afterward.

In May, writing in fervent self-defense, disputing each of Graham's claims, she complained that the experience had turned her hair white:

> *George Graham gave his wife the blessed luxury of an immediate death. To the victims of his treachery and deceit, he has awarded a torture as exquisite in its anguish as it is slow in its consummation.*[15]

For two years, Emma and Cora Lee Graham were kept on tenterhooks. Emma had to return to Missouri several times for legal proceedings that added no new evidence. In low spirits and poor health, her usefulness in temperance work badly impaired, she blamed the influence of the powerful liquor industry for the whole affair. She even took extreme measures to try to prove that Sarah Graham was not dead, but survived in the West.[16]

A low point of Emma's life came in July, 1886, when she had returned to South Bend, to the house on Marion Street, to her father and stepmother, to her half-brothers and half-sisters, who were now adults, in an effort to recuperate before facing more proceedings in Springfield.

News came from LaPorte that her son Frank, a bright fifteen-year-old who had been attending a special summer school on Fargher's Island at Pine Lake, had drowned in a boating accident. Emma wrote a poem for the *South Bend Tribune*, "Desolation," one of whose verses was as follows:

There's a weary wail in the wind;
The days are leaden, and joy has fled;
Hope lies prostrate, ambition is dead;
My life to despair seems strangely wed,
There's something I cannot find! [17]

Frank's funeral at South Bend's Milburn Chapel was attended by hundreds of people from both South Bend and LaPorte. He was buried in South Bend City Cemetery, close to Emma Molloy's mother and Emma's other children, Lottie and Allie. [18]

One afternoon in early September, after suffering all day with a sick headache, and having taken large doses of ether, Emma ran down the bank back of her father's house and plunged into the St. Joseph River. In her disturbed state, she thought she saw Frank in the water, calling out to her for help. She was rescued and put under a doctor's care. Many papers reported it as a suicide attempt. [19]

From this low point, she slowly began to recover, and in early 1887 she traveled all the way to Washington Territory. Claiming at first to be coming west to search for Sarah Graham, she brought much controversy with her, in both the daily and the Methodist press. But giving successful revivals at Victoria and Port Townsend, then a leading West coast port, she made converts and new friends. [20]

Later that year, she traveled to places where she had lived and worked, painstakingly gathering references on her moral character to present to the authorities. A few who responded, in addition to friends in the West, were Mary Livermore, Frances Willard, the Indiana WCTU, singer James G. Clark, Emile Cary, Clement Studebaker of South Bend, and Edward Molloy.

In its published resolution, the Indiana WCTU, meeting at Richmond in May, 1887, wrote in part: "...we, the women of Indiana, assembled in annual convention...learn with deep sorrow that one of our most able and faithful workers, Mrs. Emma Molloy, is being cruelly misrepresented and slandered...We desire to vindicate her character by the assurance that we believe in her, sympathize with her and trust her..." [21]

10
THE EVANGELIST
1888-1907

In 1888, finally cleared with Cora Lee Graham of all charges, Emma Molloy moved with her daughter Etta to Port Townsend, Washington. That year female suffrage had been enacted in Washington Territory, though it would turn out not to be permanent. Vowing to spend the rest of her life working for "religion and temperance," Emma succeeded in establishing for herself a useful and absorbing new life.

At the Seamen's Bethel, a mission for sailors, she preached, counseled, gave temperance talks, arranged entertainments—even giving dramatic readings herself, and once playing the guitar in a trio with zither and harmonica—and helped raise funds to keep it going.

She also became president of the local WCTU and helped bring temperance speakers to Port Townsend. Most importantly, despite some lingering controversy which diminished over time, her work in the churches grew. She not only attended the Methodist church in Port Townsend, but often preached there in the minister's absence. And her traveling evangelical work continued and expanded.[1]

Though she herself had lost much, her faith continued to be a source of strength. And at Port Townsend she at last truly found the home she had so badly needed. In the fall of 1888, with help from her new friends, she built a house at 34 Learned Avenue. Very shortly afterward, in early 1889, came her third marriage, to her old friend and cousin, Morris Barrett, who moved to Port Townsend and worked as a printer on the *Port Townsend Leader*.

Morris Barrett was described as a quiet, retiring person who evidenced great devotion to the church after Emma won him over in the course of a revival. His first wife had died, and his son, Clarence F. Barrett, was a civil servant living in Columbus, Ohio. According to an account of his marriage to Emma, the two had been engaged in their youth.

Harriet L. Adams, a traveling WCTU organizer who earlier had corresponded with Emma, stayed for a time at the Barrett home in Port

Townsend. She found Morris "in full sympathy with his wife's works and views." And she noted, "Their house is always open to those in want, whether physical or mental." One whom they took in for a few years was Daniel Dale, an elderly friend in poor health, who had rented Emma the property for her house.[2]

As years passed, Emma Molloy Barrett settled into a regular routine, spending the warmer months in Port Townsend and setting out on trips the rest of the year to evangelize in various parts of Washington, Oregon, British Columbia, and finally California. No doubt she stopped whenever possible on her travels to visit her daughter Etta, who late in 1888 had married Decatur Blakeney and lived with her growing family in Baker City, Oregon.

Though not officially appointed an evangelist by the Methodist conferences, Emma worked primarily in Methodist churches, especially in building up struggling churches in small towns. Enthusiastic accounts of the work of "Mrs. E. M. Barrett" appeared often in the Methodist journals. Illnesses still dogged her, and travel could be arduous.

But she achieved solid results, usually after working daily in a church for several weeks. In 1893, at Olympia, fifty-four people were converted in a five-week ministry. At Everett that year, membership in the Methodist church was up from forty-seven to one hundred, largely because of her efforts. At Spokane in March, 1895, after six weeks' work there were 187 conversions.[3]

In her evangelism, she placed much value upon measuring up to divine standards, yet typically emphasized,

...it is not his will that any should perish.[4]

A favorite sermon was entitled, "Thou art weighed in the balance and found wanting." In another, using an appropriate travel metaphor, she divided Christians into "first-class passengers" who "live in the assurance of faith," "second-class passengers" who are "faint-hearted Christians," and "third-class" or "automaton Christians." Salvation was "the inheritance of all God's true children." She added,

*Of course, if we ride first class we must pay the price.
It is unconditional surrender of all that separates from
God.*[5]

Never a fundamentalist, she told one congregation,

*The infidelity that is hurting the world to-day is not
the Tom Paine or the Ingersoll kind. It is the infidelity of the people who believe this Bible but don't do one
thing it tells them, who believe in this new birth but
never seek it.*[6]

About 1895 Morris Barrett suffered paralysis from a stroke. The
Barretts took in a new young foster daughter, Bessie Birekes, to give
them needed help. In January, 1903, after a good deal of suffering,
Morris Barrett died.[7]

Emma Molloy Barrett kept up her work in Methodist churches.
In November, 1904, T. L. Jones, pastor at Amity, Oregon, wrote that
Emma was still full of her old love and enthusiasm, and had brought
their church a "glorious revival," with twenty-seven people either converted or brought back to the church, by preaching the "old time gospel."

In early April, 1906, she was evangelizing in Yuba City, Califor-
nia, and may very well have felt the tremors of the great San Francisco
Earthquake on April 18. A few months later, she rented her house at
Port Townsend and set out for a long tour of Nevada and California.[8]

In May 1907, during a stagecoach trip from Susanville to
Cedarville, California, the coach was disabled, and she sat up all night
in wet clothes. She arrived at Cedarville exhausted and ill, but after
resting for a day, forced herself to get up and deliver her sermon. Shortly
after returning to bed, she went into a coma, and on May 14, died of
pneumonia at the age of sixty-seven.[9]

At her funeral at the Methodist church in Port Townsend, the
pastor spoke of the "great good" done by Emma Molloy Barrett in her
western work. Jeremiah McKean, a longtime friend and fellow evangelist, praised her and her work as well. She was buried next to Morris

Barrett at Red Man Cemetery in Port Townsend.[10]

In her will of 1906, Emma Molloy Barrett directed that her personal papers be burned. She left several hundred dollars and personal treasures to her daughter Etta Blakeney, her foster daughters Cora Lee Juel and Bessie Birekes Thomas, and friends at Port Townsend. She left family photographs, including a picture of the 1879 family reunion at Conesus Lake, New York, to her stepson, Clarence F. Barrett.

She gave just five dollars apiece to her two surviving half-brothers, William E. Barrett of Grand Rapids, Michigan, and John C. ("Tony") Barrett of South Bend, owner of an opulent saloon, "The Owl," located just a short distance north of the site of her late father's jewelry store on Michigan Street. Among her belongings were a parlor organ and pictures of Jesus Christ, the English prison reformer Elizabeth Fry, and the Greek goddess Diana.[11]

Emma's friends in Port Townsend installed a stained glass window in her memory at Trinity Church, where she had so often preached, and had been a faithful member as well for nearly twenty years. It is called the "Hope Window," and includes figures of an anchor and a lily.[12]

Edward Molloy lived the rest of his life in LaPorte, well beloved as a veteran newspaper editor, public speaker, and booster of civic and Republican Party causes. He never remarried. The *Indiana Magazine of History* found him worthy of an obituary at his death in 1914.[13]

Etta Molloy Blakeney named her eldest daughter Emma, and carefully saved a picture of her adoptive mother which was passed down through three generations to her great-grandchildren, who still admire it today.

11
In Summary

Emma Molloy Barrett had lived a pioneering life, witnessed dramatic events in history, made a striking appearance on the national stage, and when fame betrayed her, still continued her life's work with determination and success. Finding purpose from youth onward in "doing," she exemplified the strength of the "work ethic" in nineteenth-century America. She once wrote,

> *Only lazy people trust to chance in anything in this world, and laziness I consider one of the unpardonable sins.*[1]

This philosophy of work, in turn, was based on her bedrock belief in duty, that

> *...there are three things man can never escape from—conscience, record and God.*[2]

This most definitely applied to women as much as to men. As a feminist, she was impatient with the notion of female frailty, which both hindered and protected women from the sort of commitment to work she practiced.

Yet her abiding passion to be of help to others, which was only strengthened by all the adversities she faced, went far beyond a sense of duty. She once wrote,

> *Never in all my life have I failed to put out my hand helpfully to the outcast, and the unfortunate, or to speak a word of hope to the erring.*[3]

And of course her efforts to be of help went beyond help, to actually facilitating change in others. She was fired not only by a sense of Christian duty and altruism but also by enthusiasm, ambition, and determination. And unlike many women then and now, she herself made changes when things were not satisfying. She acted, to use a modern phrase, as an empowered woman.

She was notable for the breadth of her interests and her sheer versatility. Temperance, women's rights, and Christian evangelism were all of crucial importance. Through her writings, speeches, and sermons, and through personal counseling and teaching, she worked continually at the "grass roots" level to inspire the ordinary man and woman to improve their lives.

She also helped articulate the ideals of the organizations she represented, and put a radicalizing pressure on them through her dual career of journalism and activism. Dedicated workers such as Emma helped prepare for the later success of the Prohibition and Woman Suffrage movements.

WILLIAM L. BARRETT.

William Lovell Barrett, Emma's father.

Emma's stepmother, Harriett Eaker Barrett.

Three houses of the Barrett family, on the north side of the 100 block of E. Marion St., South Bend, c. 1900-1930. At left is the home William L. Barrett built for his family in the early 1850s.

Courtesy Northern Indiana Historical Society

This large wooden sign hung at William Barrett's jewelry store on Michigan St. in South Bend.

Personal collection of J. Barrett Guthrie

Zilpha "Dee" Barrett Hogue, Emma's eldest half-sister, with her daughter, Edith Adean.

Courtesy Northern Indiana Historical Society

South Bend c. 1860, looking north along Michigan St. Intersecting is Colfax Ave. (then called Market St.). The First National Bank and John Brownfield store were on the two corners. Willam Barrett's jewelry store was on the west side of Michigan just south of the buildings shown.

Courtesy Indiana Division, Indiana State Library

Edward Molloy, Emma's second husband, as a young lieutenant in the 87th Regiment, Indiana infantry.

Personal collection of the Rev. George M. Minnix

Robert K. Brush, Elkhart's postmaster, joined the Molloys as a partner in publication of the *Elkhart Observer*.

Courtesy Northern Indiana Historical Society

The Molloys' advertisement from *Turner's South Bend Directory*, 1871-72.

Engraving of Emma Molloy, from a British temperance journal, the *Good Templars' Watchword,* October 9, 1878. It also appeared that year in *The Ribbon Workers*, a biographical work by James Hiatt. It appears to have been based on her photograph.

By permission of the British Library

Drawing of Elkhart postoffice on the north side of Jackson St. west of Main, c. 1875. The *Elkhart Review* occupied the second floor, and the Molloys' *Elkhart Observer*, the basement. The building still stands, occupied by the Martin Pet & Garden store.

Courtesy Elkhart County Historical Society

Former Molloy-Graham house in Washington, Kansas, where Emma Molloy lived in 1884-85, photographed in the late 1980s. The "turret" was originally topped by a steeple.

Recent photograph of Trinity Methodist Church, Emma's home church in Port Townsend, Washington, for the last nineteen years of her life. There have been only minor changes in the exterior of the building.

Front cover of a sensational booklet published by the *Springfield Herald* in 1886.

Photo of Emma Molloy Barrett, probably in her fifties, published along with a report of a revival in the *California Christian Advocate* in April, 1902.

Emma's oldest half-brother, William E. "Will" Barrett, became a prominent lumber dealer in Grand Rapids, Michigan and Chicago.

Emma's half-brother, John C. Barrett, owner of "The Owl" saloon in South Bend, here with his daughter, Florence M. Barrett, mother of J. Barrett Guthrie.

May Barrett was the younger of Emma's half-sisters. She never married, lived all her life in South Bend, and took care of family members. In turn, her niece, Edith Adean Hogue Piatt, took care of May in her last years.

Personal collection of J. Barrett Guthrie

Personal collection of Jean Hass

Very late photograph of Emma Molloy Barrett owned by her adopted daughter, Etta Molloy Blakeney.

Photo by Eileen Martin

Emma Molloy Barrett's tombstone, located close to the marker of her third husband, Morris Barrett, in Red Man Cemetery, Port Townsend, Washington.

PART II: SELECTED WRITINGS/ADDRESSES

Over a period of fifty years, Emma wrote many hundreds of articles, editorials, stories and poems, and delivered hundreds of addresses and sermons. A good number of these have been preserved in some form. They cover a great range of style and mood. They inform. They preach and "lecture." They confide. They stir the fancy and the emotions. They enumerate points of an argument in the most practical, down-to-earth manner. They ridicule with heavy, scornful irony or with lighthearted chuckles.

The eighteen pieces which follow were selected with the following criteria in mind, though not necessarily always in this order:

Representation of her various life stages, with typical writing styles, purposes, and concerns. Some phases are, regrettably, less well represented in print. Sermons, for example, were seldom recorded, and so less is available to choose from in her later years.

Authenticity. This is a problem with many of her published addresses, and ones that appeared less than authentic were not chosen. Of course, one can never be entirely sure of each phrase.

Historical significance. A decision has been made, for example, to include some of her longer speeches and articles, which outline important phases of her career and address a wide audience, rather than including additional short pieces, worthy of inclusion though they may be.

Effectiveness of expression. The quality of Emma's writing varied a great deal, and this is true of the items which were selected. However, an attempt has been made to present at least a few of her best pieces.

Likely interest to modern readers. The theme of feminism, for example, has been given special emphasis. Her experiences as a journalist, also, are probably more attractive to the average reader than those as a reformer, and they too have been emphasized. Some of her very flowery writing that is cloying to modern taste has been avoided.

Printable length. Writing and public speaking came easily to Emma and she often tended toward length. Due to limitations of space, many excellent longer pieces needed to be eliminated from consideration. Some of the included items have been shortened.

1
Story by Emma F. Pradt,
North Iowa Times, October 12, 1859

In her early years as a writer, Emma followed the example of many other female authors in writing short stories for publication in newspapers. This one, submitted when she was twenty and married just over a year, reflects a bright, happy mood. It paints an engaging picture of life at a girls' "college" and yesterday's equivalent of the modern "singles' scene," complete with "personal" ads. The story very possibly may contain autobiographical elements, and reflects many of Emma's values.

Answering an Advertisement:
How Mollie Munson Found a Husband.

While at Union Springs Female College,[1] Mollie Munson was my room-mate, my confidant, and bosom friend. She was a wild, impetuous girl, of a frank, open nature and I really loved her with all my heart. At an early age she had lost her mother, and her father, after remaining a widower about thirteen years, married again. Mollie's step-mother was her opposite in almost every respect; so much so that her position at home was by no means an enviable one. After considerable persuasion, she at length obtained her father's consent, and became a student at Union Springs College, where an acquaintance with her commenced, which soon ripened into friendship.

Mollie determined not to return to her home, to remain any great length of time, but resolved to apply for a situation as a teacher in the G— Academy, immediately upon the expiration of her collegiate course.

We were seated one day in our room, each busy with letters and papers from home and our respective friends. Mollie had just opened a paper, and after glancing over it, burst into a fit of immoderate laughter.

"What pleases you so much, Mollie?" I asked.

"Oh, Nelly! Did you ever! Here's a paper, called the 'Ledger of Romance,'[2] with '*Matrimonial Advertisements*' in it!—Here's the picture of a pretty good looking fellow. He says he has a fortune, consisting of a valuable plantation near Richmond, and a plenty of money—is a gentleman by birth and education, and, as a matter of course, he belongs to the 'F. F. V.'s.' Bah! He has a mighty good opinion of himself.—But here is another. 'A young man of respectability, engaged in a lucrative business, wishes to marry a prudent, economical wife—one calculated to make home happy, and who would love and be contented with a man in moderate circumstances. His wife must be a helpmate and a friend. Address Henry Fontaine, Horicon, Wis.' Now, Nellie, he's the stuff for me, and I'm going to answer that advertisement."

"I wouldn't, Mollie. You don't know who or what he is. I wouldn't run the risk."

"Pshaw! there's no risk. My answering the advertisement is no sign that I am going to marry him. So, here goes."

Seating herself at her writing desk, she commenced the epistle. For a few moments her gold pen almost flew over the paper; then stopping and drawing a long breath, she exclaimed:

"There, now. 'By the ghost of Moll Kelly,' as Pat says, I've gone and done it."[3]

"Well, read your tender missive, Mollie."

"Very well," she replied; "let the audience give me their strict and undivided attention, and I will proceed."

Then giving two or three very dramatic and pompous "Ahems!" she began:

"Mr. Fontaine—*Dear Sir*: Your letter in the 'Ledger of Romance' has just met my eye; and as it just suits me, I have determined to answer it. Whether I should be an economical wife or not, I am not prepared to say; but I believe I am not extravagant. I think I would be very well suited 'with love in a cottage.' So, if you desire it, I will commence a correspondence with you on this subject, Address Miss Mollie Munson, Union Springs, Ala."

Bribing Tom, the mulatto boy, who performed the *arduous* duties of carrying letters to and from the Post Office, to mail the letter without the usual scrutiny of Miss Duplain, a spinster of *very* uncertain age, and who wore *very* long curls, and who was *very* curious—who, withal, was continually lecturing us on our deportment, and the propriety of this, that, and the other, until we fairly dreaded her approach, so sure were we of a lecture—we had the satisfaction, for once, of outwitting her.

A few weeks passed on. One day, Jim brought Mollie a letter, post-marked Horicon, directed in a bold, manly hand. It ran thus:

"Miss Munson: Your letter has just reached me, and I hasten to reply. The 'advertisement' was inserted in the 'Ledger of Romance' through a mistake on the part of the editor. I intended the *letter*—which he published as an *advertisement,* with some alterations—as an answer to an advertisement which had appeared in that paper, from a young lady. I supposed the editor would forward it to her, and that her reply would afford me some amusement. However, since you have taken it seriously, and as I am much pleased with your letter, I hope our correspondence may continue; and I trust that my own letters may prove interesting and attractive enough to heartily repay you for your trouble in writing to me. I will give you a short sketch of myself.—My parents died and left me at an early age, to combat with the world, with but few friends, and no dollars. I served an apprenticeship at the printing business, in my native town—R— F—, Va. Soon after I commenced my career as journeyman. I became acquainted with a strolling Thespian Troupe, and joined the company as their 'funny man.' On account of the objections of relations, however, I soon abandoned them, and applied for an engagement in a 'regular' theatre, at I—, as Low Comedian, which I obtained. My friends still opposing my theatrical career, I 'retired from the stage,' and became a country editor. Like most of that unfortunate class, however, I found that the profession was not as *profitable,* pecuniarily, as I could wish, and gave up my paper in disgust.—At present, I have a situation as book-keeper, in Horicon, Wis. All I need, now, to make me perfectly happy, is a nice little wife; and I hope you may, upon further acquaintance, love me well enough to supply my want. I am sure I shall love you.

Henry Fontaine."[4]

"Would you answer it, Nell?"

"Just as you choose. You will do just as you please any way. I believe I would, though, for I am half in love with him, myself, but we will discuss this subject at some other time, for it is time we went to our Algebra class."

Strange to say, Mollie failed that day, in her lesson. Miss Duplaine was surprised, as Mollie was one of her best scholars. Our recitations for the day being over, the subject was fully discussed in our room, and Mollie proceeded to answer the letter. The next week, school closed. Reader, do you remember when you parted with your school mates— left the scene of so many happy hours? The girls were busy packing their trunks, exchanging pictures, and bidding good byes. Mollie and I were to travel together as far as Columbus; our trunks, therefore, were strapped, and we were waiting for the stage, which came at last, and we commenced our journey. At Columbus, we separated. I took the morning train for Tennessee, and she the evening train for Virginia.

For nearly a year, I heard nothing more of Mollie's love affair. One morning, however, I received a letter from her, containing the news of her marriage with Henry Fontaine! She also wrote me that she and her liege lord would soon be with me for a short visit.

After anxiously watching the cars for a few days, I at length welcomed them to my home. We all enjoyed the visit famously. Mollie persuaded me to accompany them to their home in Wisconsin, where I spent the remainder of the summer very pleasantly.

When we arrived at Horicon, Henry sent a wedding card to the *Argus* office. Mr. Pomeroy, the editor,[5] inserted an elaborate and highly complimentary puff, which was written in his characteristic style. Whether the "bountiful supply of rich wedding cake," and the "basket of sparkling Catawba, fit for the Gods," had anything to do with the puff, I have never learned.

Henry and Mollie are enjoying as great an amount of wedded bliss as usually falls to the lot of mortal beings.

Reader, you have learned "how Mollie Munson found a husband."

2

Poem by Emma F. Pradt,
Wisconsin Evening Patriot, February 25, 1862

*Despite the hopeful mood of "Answering an Advertisement" and some
of her other early writings, the young Emma Pradt also wrote often of the
capacity of life to disappoint or destroy youthful dreams of happiness.*

Soul-Clouds and Soul-Light.

Lost, lost, lost, a beautiful gladsome dream:
Lost, forever lost, on Time's relentless stream;
Oh! how I loved it, cherished and blessed it;
Oh! how my young heart wildly caressed it;
Yet it is gone, and alone in my sorrow,
I wildly, though vainly, hope that to-morrow,
With its gay sunlight, its birds, and bright flowers,
Will bring me the visions of happier hours.

Lost, lost, lost,—wrecked on the shoals of Life—
Lost 'mid its perilous breakers—the strife
Of the billows have borne them away—
Have carried the hopes of my girlhood's day;
Vainly the flickering torch strives to burn:
Ever, yes, ever thus, heart, must thou mourn—
No glad to-morrow—no hope, now, for thee—
Wrecked, ever wrecked, and lost, must thou be.

Found, found, found, a blessed, Eternal Rest:
Found, and forever mine—Oh! how perfectly blest!
No more repinings—no more anguish, or tears;
Found, 'though lost to me long, long years;
Treasured are they, in Heaven's archives;
Found, in the Book of Life; and o'er its leaves
The waves of oblivion never may roll;
There they are treasured—the hopes of my soul.

3
Excerpt from Essay by Emma F. Pradt,
North Iowa Times, September 23, 1863

In this more "chatty" piece, Emma Pradt remembered with a nostalgic glow, and much descriptive detail, some of her childhood experiences in the home of George and Martha Bryson. She noted a strong contrast with her present life.

The Old Home.

...My first remembrances are of the dear old front room with its white muslin curtains, its neat, rag carpet and flag bottomed chairs; the mantle over which hung the pictures of "Burns[6] and his Highland Mary" and Presidents, with Washington in the centre. Then the sitting room, with the old clock whose friendly tic-tack, told the quiet moments as they peacefully glided by. That old clock was a great marvel to me, for upon its door was paintings of fashionable beaux and belles of fifty years ago, with bonnets that rose high and grand in front (a *little* worse than the present style) and sleeves that looked as though they might have contained a pillow or so. Then "Grandma" would tell how she once had a dress made of beautiful French calico and how she wore it to a corn husking the first time.

Then there was the old cherry table, whereon I wrote my first essay for the village school, the dresser in the marvelously neat kitchen, with its row of bright pans upon it, and within the blue ware with such beautiful pictures on them. I'd rather drink tea to-day from one of those cups, reader, than one of the most costly China, and the cherry table would be far more valuable to me than the most elegant marble-topped mahogany. I can remember distinctly my perfect happiness when in the long quiet summer afternoons Grandma sat with her work basket before her fixing something for "that dear child" while I sat on Grandpa's knee in the vine covered porch reading to him, for he had been perfectly blind many years. Long weary years have passed since then and in distant climes have I wandered; I have gathered to my heart many dear friends, but no voice has ever fallen on my heart so sweetly as the voices of the old couple praying "God to bless that dear child." I know now that *their* hearts were *true* and no meed of praise or word of adulation can ever sound as sweet as the chiming of the memory-bells whispering the fond prayer, *"God bless that dear child!"*

They still live, reader; the old cottage is still just about the same with a few improvements. Nothing scarcely is changed except the gay happy child of fifteen years ago. She has grown from the careless child to the world-weary, care-worn woman; life's bright flowers faded and the glad leaping joy-fountains dried. Oh! for one hour of that blessed childhood, when the heart might forget its burden of care and the hollowness and deceit of the world and enjoy the love of the true hearts that blessed me then.

4
Excerpts from Essay by Emma F. Pradt,
Wisconsin Patriot, December 31, 1863

A few weeks after her daughter Lottie's death, Emma again sat down to remember, and wrote this somber and ornate expression of grief to share with her readers. Allie, too, would be lost in just a few more months.

New Year's Eve.

New Year's Eve, and once more I watch December, as she clasps cold hands with January, gathering up her robe, gemmed with frost-pearls, and glides swiftly away, leaving the year to its burial. Sunny, joyous Spring! beautiful Summer! glorious Autumn! all laid in the golden urn of sixty-three.

I am trying, in this dreamy twilight, to sum up the past blessed yet sad year, while the tic-tac of the clock tells me how fast the hours of the dying year are being numbered.

With its first hours came our little ALLIE, with his innocent life baptizing my soul with the choicest, holiest joy of womanhood; and as I gathered my pearls to my heart, how I thanked the All Father, that I was deemed worthy to wear them.

October—glorious gorgeous October—came, and when the leaves began to fall, and the hills put on their hazy crown, fearful, awful desolation was written on our lintel: for the feet of our little LOTTIE went down into the cold river. Spring will come, with her same old, yet ever new lesson, wakening the sweet blue-eyed violet, and the golden butter-cup; but the little hand that this year gathered them, will not grasp them. It is stiff and fast: Death holds it.

The gooseberry bush sways in the night-wind. It holds a shred of her dress, caught by its thorny hand, as she romped by, in her wild merriment. What matters it? She will never wear it more. Sadly we look for her in the old, accustomed garden walks. She will never, never tread them more. The "winter sifts its snow" upon the little mound where we have laid our darling...

... My baby, ALLIE, sleeps at my feet, the blessed sleep of childhood. How I long to look into his future, and see if all his New Years will be happy ones. Not all, though, for death and sorrow walk always at our side. God help us when they visibly appear unto us.

Is my New Year's greeting a sad one, reader? Well, it has eased my aching heart to come to you in my sorrow. This will be read in bright homes, where desolation has not come, thank God; and in others, where its shadow has fallen, it will waken the warm tear of sympathy.

To all, then, a bright, unshadowed, peaceful, happy New Year.

5

Satirical Essay by Emma F. Pradt, writing as "Polly Wiggins," *Wisconsin Capitol,* March 14, 1866

In sharp contrast to her writings that draw on personal sorrows, are those that look outward on the changing scenes of history. In Madison, Emma Pradt became skilled as a reporter through such experiences as visiting the theatre and the State Fair, and sitting attentively in the visitors' gallery of the state legislative chambers. Through adopting the character of "Polly Wiggins," she not only reported but also offered a good share of satiric commentary. The "Polly Wiggins" letters, beginning in August, 1865, became so popular that a bill was indeed introduced in the legislature to buy her postage stamps and stationery. Writing in "fractured" English was a lively tradition of the time among both male and female humorists. It is possible that in writing about the legislature she was inspired by the successful writer Jane Swisshelm, who had spoken at Madison.

This letter to her "Kuzzin Mehitable" describes a session of the Wisconsin State Senate on March 7, 1866.

Madison, March 13th.

Dere Mehit.:[7]

I have actooally had a bill up in the legislater. Yew may say what yew plese about "woman's spere," and awl that nonsense. I ges awl yew folks in Punkinville will open your ise when yew git the paper I send yew with Polly Wiggins' bill. I'll tell yew how it awl cum around. Me and wun of my sity frends went up to the Assembly chamber last Wensday. The parsun was just prayin, but the members were not emprest as I thot they shood be. Wun of 'em wuz a whittelin a pine stick with grate enthoosyasm; another was peroosin a bill to prevent miners playin bilyards. He sed the grown folks dident stand a shadder of a chanse tew get a billyard tabel in this wicked sity, bekause the young fri so monoppolized it. Wun of the reporters of the Jurnal[8] was hurriedly peroosin a pile of papers as if he dident expect tew hev another minit in ten years. When the parsin had konkluded they rusht frantickly around as though they had got fleas in their eers. After thay had most awl of em had a say about matters and things, and the billyard bill had been considered, Mister Raymind[9] riz with his benevolent feechers awl aglow, and presented a bill tew "furnish Polly Wiggins ten dollars wuth of postig stamps."

We had some fealin speaches on the subjeckt. An onest, well-meanin skule-teacher from Racine kounty sed he wuz "ashamed of the proceedins of this boddy." I wundered if he wood hev bin if the stamps had bin fur him. It is astonishin how folks dew differ. Now that appeared tew me the most sensibel of enney bill thay kould present, and while my hart wus all glowin with enthoosyasim and I wuz a fealin as ef I had "struck ile" or sprung a "Kalleyforney" or "Pike's Peak" gold vane, Jack Turner got up and proposed sinse sum members wuz inklined tew make sich a fuss about it, to raise the stamps by private contribushin. That ef Mr. Hadley[10] wood furnish ten dollers wurth of stationary he wood furnish the stamps. Mr. H. riz in grate konsternashin violently klutchin his pockets, and with falterin voice and teerful eyes beseeched the members not tew draw on him tew strong fynancialy, as he had no more munny than wood settel his onest dets. He then bust intew flites of eloquence and sublime orretory far beyond my understandin kapacity. Thare we sot tew mortal hours, listenin to his defense; not that he said so much, but he repeeted evry wurd over twice for fear we shood not understand, and when he got threw and sot down, wipin the sweat off his venerabel ferred, we knode less than when he begun, and I kum to the konklushin that though he wuz a very perlite and genial old gentleman, speech-makin was not wun of his 4ts. The house then referred it tew a seleckt kommitty of tew, Mister Turner and Mr. Hadley. I havent seen the stamps, but when I git em I shall feel so rich I kan rite yew tew letters a week, and Josh sez in vew of savin so much postig, I shal hav a new dress, as my red and yaller silk dress is most wore out.

When this wuz disposed of, the semetery bill[11] kum up. A dockter sumbody of Milwaukee got up and made a touchin speech. He sed in New York folks kould inter *enny* of their friends in the church yards. (I am glad I dont live thare for I dont want tew be intered before I am dead.) He said he dident sea how the juse of five dead boddys was goin tew hurt wun well, specially when they wuz enkased in butiful mahogony coffins, and a water lime sement severil feet thick wuz around them, and a large stone wayin severil tuns, certinly wood prevent the speerits risin tew disturb the widder in the ded hours of the nite. It wuz quite a quary in my mind whether the parsun hadent got his wife berryed so tite that Gabriel would have tew give her a special toot in pretty close quarters, for her tew hear. What a pity it wood be for her tew be burryed so as to be left out in the kold on akkount of not hearin, and after the laps of so many years the parsun in kountin up his numerous wives might forgit her intirely! The widder, I understand has got a majority, and so when the Parsin transplants his numerous family again I hope thay will put a smaller stone over em.

A noin friend, Mehit, hez told me what kind of a thing a LOBBY is, and i wunder thay don't have one in the circus. Though what the performers, and clown and ringmaster wood du, if it pulled 'em round by the nose as it does the Legislatur, I can't tell. But there it wouldn't du enney harm, while tha tell me its powerful damagin to the people for it tu run the Legislatur. It hez got more heds and horns than the beest in Scriptoor. I am told it hez at least ten horns[12] a day for every member, and tha may be had at a private room in the Valise House.[13] It is ginnerally found sittin near the fense, (on the inside,) that keeps gentlemen sepparated from members. Mister Chandler,[14] in the Senit, took a heavy drive at it, the uther da, but in (*sic*) krowds in jest as klose es ever. It hez got the slickest tung! It charms em ez Josh charmed my effecshinit and pantin' hart. It iz wunderful rich, I'm told, but a sort of bloo beard that is onhelthy for a begiled mortal to get in its claw. Ime told tho that Jack Turner is too much for it, as his name sake wuz for the jient. Ile tell you more about the critter ez I lern more.

But, law me, here I've got and rit tew yew until the teekettel is biled dry as a bone and the pork and beans is awl burnt tew a sinder, and Josh will be in direcktly, givin me Hail Kolumbia for not tendin tew my household dutys. Josh gits a leetle kross sumtimes, but he is a good feller, enny way. I have jist herd sumthin rich, but havent time tew rite till the next letter.

Yewrs, for the Legislater,

POLLY WIGGINS.

6

Essay by Emma Molloy,
South Bend National Union, December 21, 1867

When Emma returned to South Bend and divorced Louis Pradt, her
fortunes changed. Marrying Edward Molloy and going to work for the
National Union *offered seemingly umlimited chances for satisfaction and*
fulfillment, despite a life that was financially precarious.

Among the early opportunities she seized as editorial writer was to put
forward her strong opinions on responsible motherhood and household
economy. This piece was written not long after her marriage to Edward
Molloy and assumption of the post of junior editor. Parallels might easily be
drawn with today's tendencies toward overspending. Thrown in, too, was
a forceful condemnnation of gossip, seen often in Emma's writing.

The Insincerity of Social Life.

"Come and see me, do now;" a little hypocritical kiss, and the two
ladies separate, while the Recording Angel has one more society lie on
his book. At your friend's solicitation, some day, being in a social mood,
you call. Your heart is in its sunniest state. As it expands its tendrils
reach out after the good and pure in your friend's nature. The time glides
pleasantly by, and you are astonished to find that your few minutes call
has lengthened itself into a half hour. You go home feeling that this is
a pleasant world and that Mrs. D— is a dear, delightful woman.

Next week you hear of your call something after this wise: "Mrs.
J— called on me last week.—She had on a horrid shabby bonnet, and
her old merino dress turned and made over. Wonder why Mr. J— don't
dress her better? She looks genteel, its true, but she ought to be a little
more up with the times. By the way, did you ever hear that Mrs. J—
was disappointed in love? No?" Well—an ominous shake of the head
follows, which might mean four or five hundred different things—and
the story goes on, until, when your friend (?) is done with your past
history and character, and has it dissected to her satisfaction, you take
it up, and look it over, and fail to recognize anything familiar in it.

Now, in general, running after society is just this saw-dust sort of stuff. No nutriment—no life-giving, healthful draught, as it should be. There is too much trying to appear what we are not, starving the larder to bedeck the "outer man"—too much whitewashing without, when "within is rottenness and dead men's bones."

A foolish mother lets Willie go with leaky shoes that she may procure an expensive Honiton collar[15] to wear to Mrs. M—'s party.— The consequence is Mrs. M— wonders where Mrs. R— got it, if it was paid for, and, ten to one, says to her intimate friend: "I don't see how, with their small income and large family, Mrs. R— dresses so expensively," &c., *ad infinitum*. But this does not end it. Willie wakes the thoughtless, but really affectionate mother up in the night with the croup. A few hours of anguish, a wringing of heart-strings and the death angel has relieved little Willie of life's weary load. Friends strive to comfort the heart-broken mother with the assurance that "God took her little angel home." Now this laying the foolishness and pride of humanity with its consequences to God is simply absurd. It was the mother's thoughtless vanity that cost her the child's life, and not "God's mysterious providence." For the eyes of a thoughtless crowd, who, in her bereavement, hardly give her a passing thought, she bedecked herself in the costly robe of her innocent child's life.—These are the husks of society.

A young couple enter upon the sea of matrimony. They are poor, but the custom of society demands a long and expensive wedding trip, costly bridal outfits, &c. It would not do to neglect this requirement, "for what would folks say?" What follows? When they return their resources are so diminished that they have scarcely a dollar with which to commence house-keeping. The young husband is thus so early thrown in debt, and it would only be a wonder, if in a dozen years thereafter he is not a broken-spirited man, still in debt, with a group of little children dependent upon him, and a discontented, unhappy wife for a partner.

If there is any one thing that I am entirely out of patience with, it is this extreme sensitiveness about poverty. It is simply evidence of a vulgar, uncultured mind. I cannot conceive of the man, who has any thing noble in his nature, any self respect, any real elevation of character, yielding to this low-born shame. It is—mark it well wherever you find it—the sure indication of an inferior mind. Is not genius, genius still, though it be clothed in rags? or, as Carlyle[16] expresses it: "Is not God within the head, tho' a torn skull cap be without?" Then people talk about being slighted, as if any one ever could be slighted unless he slighted himself. True, Mrs. So and So may attempt to do it by mak ing a large party and inviting your more prosperous neighbor, but, if your mind is well balanced, the shaft will have no barb. If you suffer from it I think it's because you have not the right stamina—have not learned to depend on your own centre of gravity. Learn to have self poise enough, my young friend—enough largeness of soul—to refrain from extravagance which you cannot afford, simply because it is dishonest to strive to appear what you are not. "Life is real and earnest"[17]—an ever springing fountain—a great deep—never fathomed—never bounded. It is full of singing birds and glad sunbeams, if you only know how to catch the music and the sunshine. The secret is in living so nobly, so justly, and with such dignity, that the insincerity of social life shall fail to contaminate.

7
Advertisement by Emma Molloy, *South Bend National Union*, July 25, 1868

Handling much writing and editing with merciless deadlines, Emma Molloy learned to make her newspaper copy crisp, interesting and entertaining to read. One method was by the use of humor. This short piece describes her search for a hired girl who would ease her arduous workday. It was followed in a later issue by a piece detailing the interviewing of prospective candidates. Her viewpoint in both was influenced by her previous difficulty in finding reliable household help.

The Editress of this paper wishes to hire a girl. Finding the duties of house and office too numerous to be accomplished in the short period of from 12 to 15 hours a day, she would like to have some professor-ess of the dish-rag persuasion, show herself at this office immediately. One not particular about sleeping in the spare bedroom, or wearing her employers dresses preferred.

It is also quite desirable that she should not expect her employer to make the beds, sweep, wipe dishes and help do the washing Mondays previous to going to the office to work.

A girl with red hair not desired as hair of that color is rather unpleasant in the pie or soup, but if a person of the above named kind present herself the subject will receive consideration.

The Editress wishes to say also that she has had her stock of dishes insured, therefore a careful person will be no object! - though a person in the habit of breaking more than one set a week need not apply.

A girl with some idea of breadbaking, and who can cook a steak without someone standing beside her to turn it preferred, though one not possessed of these accomplishments can spend the time very pleasantly, while her employer is performing the above mentioned duties, by playing with the cat or reading one of Beadle's dime novels.[18]

In fact most any kind of a girl who does not feel too much above her business to do a small share of the housework, for the sum of two dollars a week, may hear of something to her advantage, by calling at this office and enquiring for the Editress.

8

Excerpts from an Article by Emma Molloy,
South Bend National Union, August 8, 1868

*Filling the columns of the paper with interesting matter without a staff
of reporters was often a challenge. Since Emma enjoyed travel, and writing
came easily, many of her lengthy travel pieces enlivened the pages of the*
National Union *and the Molloys' later paper, the* Elkhart Observer. *They
ranged from descriptions of nearby towns, with profiles of their residents, to
sketches of the life of large cities. Emma was still scribbling these pieces years
later, at the height of her temperance career. The travel description below,
which has been excerpted because of its great length, was written when the
Molloys visited New York to attend a Democratic veterans' convention connected with the 1868 Presidential campaign.*

Our First Visit to New York.
A Hoosier's Views of Gotham.

...Oh! wasn't it hot. Politicians stood in little groups before their
several headquarters, earnestly discussing the chances of their favorites, wiping energetically the streams of perspiration that were making little furrows through the dust on their faces. Old ladies sat anxiously eyeing their fruit stands on the corners, where the flies were
seasoning dirty looking slices of pineapple, and billious looking mo-
lasses candy. The weary looking horses plodding over the hot cobble
stones, dragging the crowded street car after them, would have excited
the commiseration of any one but a New Yorker.

Some one said "let's go to Jones' Woods[19] and see the
Schutzenfest." So thitherward we wended our way. Here such a scene
met the eye as only a German crowd can produce. The ground arranged
like a vast theatre, scores of men in gorgeous and quaint costumes—
Tyrolese peasantry, mingling with Prussian grenadiers, carrying flint-
lock muskets of the time of Frederick the Great, smiling at the Teuton
warriors clad in grotesque suits of bearskin, portly looking dames with
hot looking babies surveying the scene with pride and satisfaction, the
whole crowd laughing, talking, and enjoying themselves as only a

German crowd can.

The banquet room was one hundred and seventy feet long by one hundred wide, beautifully decorated with flags and floral devices. At the farther end of the hall was a stand from which the toasts were announced and responded to. The shields of all the States were displayed upon the walls.

A large shed had been erected for the accommodation of those who were to compete for the prizes. Fifty-six rests were placed in range with a like number of targets, which were arranged at a distance of six hundred feet. At these positions the marksmen now take their places, and at the signal boom of the cannon the firing commences. During the excitement, a piercing wail rings out from the opposite side of the 'grounds.' The crowd rush to the spot and discover that a bullet has pierced the target board, and it is feared fatally injured an infant in its mother's arms. The poor half distracted woman is conveyed home in a carriage and our sport is spoiled here for today, so we start for Central Park.

How shall we begin to describe this beautiful marvel of nature and art combined?

It contains not far from a thousand acres of land and is called Central Park from its central position on Manhattan Island, and there is not a doubt in the mind of any Gothamite but this will one day be the centre of the metropolis. Entering from Fifth Avenue we stroll down the smooth winding paths, across a rustic bridge, and presently find ourselves in front of the "casino," a building of the Italian villa style, and a beautiful, as well as useful, ornament to the Park; for within are dispensed to invalids artificial mineral waters with all the healing properties of Kissengen, Congres, Seltzer and Vichy Springs. This building was erected at a cost of $30,000. Just back of the Mineral Spring Pavilion is a fine statue of Burns and his friend taking the parting drink for "Lang Syne."

Farther down we enter the children's playhouse, where we seat ourselves to rest for a few moments, and listen to the music of Dudworth's band, as the tender melody of "Ueber Land und Meer" ripples out on the evening air, and watch the crowds that promenade the "Mall." The beauties of the scene are as free to the poor tired laborer who stops with his dinner pail in hand to rest on the cool fragrant grass as to the millionare who rolls by in his superb equipage. Here all classes meet and mingle in the moving mass of humanity, breathing hearty blessings upon the "City Fathers" for the privileges of Central Park, with its arsenal where all of nature's wonders are gathered, its unexpected grottoes, the "Cave," the camel, the miniture lake, with its innumerable cool retreats, and its happy looking swans, its huge reservoir, &c.

We enter a jaunty little Gondola and enjoy a delightful ride on the lake, with the willows long sprays and bright fragrant flowers kissing its waters near the shore. I remarked to "Pat:"[20] "It is astonishing to me that human nature which so loves to tear to pieces, break, deface and destroy, should be so *saintly* in New York that the flowers bloom untouched, and the rabbits and squirrels fearlessly wander through these grounds, unmolested by the sacreligious hand of even a stray newsboy!

"It's the perlice mum," suggests our young friend at the oar.

Just then one of these blue coated, white gloved gents stepped out from a small copse, as a bright-eyed little chap was apparently meditating upon the chances of picking a tempting looking rose that was nodding its pinky cheek to him. Somehow, I wished the little fellow had got it, though I suppose it is heresy to think, much less say such a thing...

The next day, having a *penchant* for printing offices, we went into the "*Tribune* office." Our attention was directed by a friend to a portly gentleman, pleasant faced and pleasant voiced, whom we were informed was Horace Greeley, we were duly introduced, and, upon being informed that we were from South Bend, he grasped our digit with more warmth than we were prepared for, as we stood awed in the presence of one of the "Great Men of Our Times."...

We also...called at the office of the "*Revolution*," a paper advocating Womans Rights, and ably edited by Miss Susan B. Anthony and Mrs. Elizabeth Cady Stanton. Miss Anthony is a dignified gentle looking lady, and Mrs. Stanton a noble motherly looking woman of perhaps fifty years of age. We have received several copies and pronounce the "*Revolution*" up with the times and wish it and its Editresses all the success which their talents deserve...

9

Editorial by Emma Molloy,
Elkhart Observer, April 30, 1873

This thoughtful and striking editorial is a good statement of Emma Molloy's maturing perceptions of the progress women were making, the importance of the work of the trail-blazers of the movement, and the response of various men. By this time she herself had begun a lecturing career and identified fairly strongly with those women leaders. She no doubt intended it to be noticed, not only by her neighboring journalists, but also possibly by a national periodical.

About Women.

The following thoughts were suggested on hearing a remark made by a dapper little fellow who was engaged in the *very arduous* duties of measuring calico and delaine, and whose mathematical faculties are kept on the stretch by the exhausting labor of figuring up small bills of tape, pins, etc., in one of our dry goods stores. The question of woman's enfranchisement was being discussed. In a very indignant tone the intellectual youth affirmed, "When the women get to voting they had better take to wearing the breeches at once." A bright intelligent girl standing near replied, "It is not generally supposed that a man's garments do the voting, although they are almost all there is of *some* men."

We went away pondering in our mind the question whether we had ever seen a man who gave utterance to such sentiments, that was not a mawkish nobody, who seemed afraid that some woman would outstrip him in the great race of life. If he was a married man this peculiarity was particularly prominent. A late writer has said that "there is nothing a weak man likes so much as to be considered strong, nothing a hen-pecked man likes so much as to be regarded a tyrant. If you ever hear a man boast of his determination to rule his own house, you may feel sure that he is subdued. A henpecked husband always makes a great show of opposing any thing that looks toward the enlargement of the work or privileges of women. Such a man insists on the shadow of authority because he cannot have the substance. It is a great satisfaction to him that his wife can never be president, and that she cannot make speeches in prayer-meeting. While he retains these badges of superiority, he is still in some sense head of the family."

The signs of the times indicate that the age is producing men and women of a better stamp than these, but there must be a few specimens of the original preserved for the benefit of the next generation. The ancient style of women who were content to sit on a sort of pedestal, bowing over their fans at men who told them of their personal charms and the devotion they inspired, are out of date. In the age gone by girls were grown very much as the farmer prepares pigs for an agricultural show, and men felt bound to sing praises to their eyes, hands and feet, and write lovely verses in which the charms of these members were duly inventoried. Women were thus made abjectly dependent upon their physical charms, and then ridiculed for spending three fourths of their time in the endeavor to enhance them.

But in these days of reform and of the agitation of the woman question, girls begin to learn the fact that to be practical is to be independent, and to be independent is to instil new vitality to woman. *Men who are men* nowadays do not first ask the question "Is she pretty?" but it is "Does she know anything?"

Poor old Dr. Bushnell becomes alarmed.[21] The old fellow, in his dotage, begins to think that the type of woman is to be so changed that her loveliness will be destroyed. He forebodes a change in the physical type of the sex, draws a picture of a wiry, peaked-nose, lantern-jawed scare-crow, and labels it the woman politician of the 20th century, and then dares women to vote and go to primary meetings. Surely, he never saw Mrs. Stanton, with her round, chubby, good-natured face, or Mary Livermore[22] who to-day, physically, will bear comparison with any of the "lantern-jawed " politicians at Washington. We would not diminish the domestic virtues, but we do, somehow, think these women have *saved* better than they would in a daily journey from pantry to kitchen and back again, saving bits of grease and scraps of dry bread for puddings, and we can't see, for the life of us, how it is any better to grow sharp-featured under the nervous worry of the colored bow best suited to our complexion, or the size and color of the kid glove we shall wear, than under a pleasurable intellectual excitement.

This appeal to woman's vanity is an appeal to her weakness, and we must say, commend us to a man who expresses his admiration for Susan Anthony behind her grim spectacles, marshaling the working women of New York, or Anna Dickinson riding on an engine through an Iowa storm to deliver a lecture, even though they will not bear comparison with the fashionable woman freezing in January with a screen between her face and the fire to save her withered cheeks of sixty-nine; or a woman like Mrs. A. T. Stewart,[23] snarling in her marble palace over the wretched heart-hunger that is consuming her.

10
Excerpts from a Column by Emma Molloy,
Elkhart Observer, April 23, 1873

*One of the things Emma Molloy seemed to delight in was to record
and collect recipes and household advice and present them to her readers in
her homemaker's column, "The Hearthstone," which ran in the* Elkhart
Observer *beginning in April, 1873. This is a brief specimen (excerpted) of
one column, which happens to contain a vignette of her family life.*

The Housekeeper's Diary.

April 14th. I have a new method of keeping little fingers and brains
busy, which is synonymous with keeping them out of mischief as well
as happy. Children are remarkably like grown people in this respect; if
they are well employed I will risk their suffering from *ennui*, or finding time or inclination to naughtiness. The said plan is this: I give them
a "Documentary Journal" of which we have so many lying around, and
set them to making a scrapbook, not only of selections of prose and
poetry, but of pictures, cut from old magazines, and pictorial papers.
It is really astonishing what taste they display in these selections, and,
while searching for them, a fund of useful knowledge is acquired without the apparent effort of study. It is amusing to see our little two year
old Frank demurely cutting away with a pair of round pointed scissors
with which he cannot possibly injure himself, imagining that he, too,
is engaged in an important work. Then, when an hour has been passed
in making a litter, several minutes can be employed in cleaning up, thus
cultivating habits of neatness and order....

April 17th. Mary[24] has worn a pair of kid shoes all winter, and
they began to look so rusty, that we tried to devise some method of
restoring them. We took a small quantity of good black ink, mixed it
with the white of an egg, and applied it with a soft sponge. The effect
was magical.

11
Satirical Essay by Emma Molloy,
Elkhart Observer, April 30, 1873

A softer, more tongue-in-cheek specimen of Emma Molloy's feminist writing, again on the theme of women's difficult life.

A Question Answered.

Can any body tell why, when Eve was manufactured from one of Adam's ribs, a hired girl wasn't made at the same time to wait on her?—*Exchange.*

We can easily! Because Adam never came whining to Eve with a ragged stocking to be darned, a collar string to be sewed on, or a glove to be mended "right away, quick now!" Because he never read the newspaper until the sun got down behind the palm trees, and then stretched himself, yawning out, "ain't supper most ready my dear?" Not he. He made the fire and hung over the tea-kettle himself, we'll venture, and pulled the radishes, and peeled the bananas, and did everything else that he ought to do! He milked the cows and fed the chickens, and looked after the pigs himself. He never brought home half a dozen friends to dinner, when Eve hadn't any fresh pomegranates, and the mango season was over! He never staid out until eleven o'clock to a "ward meeting," for the out-and-out candidate, and then scolded because poor Eve was sitting up and crying, inside the gates. To be sure he acted rather cowardly about the apple gathering time, but that don't depreciate his general helpfulness about the garden! He never played billiards, nor drove fast horses, nor choked Eve with cigar smoke. He never loafed around corner groceries while solitary Eve was rocking the little Cain's cradle at home.

That's the reason that Eve did not need a hired girl, and we wish it was the reason why none of her descendants did.

12
Emma Molloy's Address on Women in Country Journalism,
Woman's Congress, Chicago, Illinois, October 15-17, 1874
Woman's Journal, November 28, 1874, p. 380

*A high point of Emma's early years in public life was her attendance
at the second Woman's Congress in Chicago in October, 1874. In the midst
of eminent and influential women from all over America, she had a chance
to substitute for a missing speaker. This address gives a detailed account of
how the first woman newspaper editor of northern Indiana made a success
of her endeavor, and combined it with her family life.*

FEMALE JOURNALISM.

The next paper in order was on journalism, by Mrs. Malloy, connected with the press at Elkhart, Ind.

Not until coming into the city was I aware that I was to fill any
part of the programme of this august body, and it is only because of
the illness of the gifted lady to whom this duty was assigned that a voice
from Hoosierdom is to cry in the wilderness, "Prepare ye the path for
Woman in journalism." But, ladies, I am not going to offer any apology; that would be too much like the men. I am simply going to give
you a little plain business talk, leaving the elaborations to these grand
women who are so accustomed to talking to the dear public that it has
become a sort of second nature.

When by any course of reasoning or experience Woman has succeeded in solving any problem in the great arithmetic of labor, I hold
that duty calls her to give that solution to her struggling sisterhood.
So I say, that to me, the path has been a pleasant one; and I think
Woman is pre-eminently fitted for the profession of journalism.

THE MANAGEMENT OF A COUNTRY NEWSPAPER,

especially calls out all the latent energies and all the ability, and how
many times I have looked at some of the miserable failures among our
country journalists, and prayed Heaven to raise up a few more Jane

Swisshelms, Helen Manvilles, and Dr. Ellen Fergusons[25] to deliver us from these male frauds. There are hundreds of women in America today who would be a great acquisition to the profession, and I am surprised that more are not choosing it.

Newspaper work, however, means business, and a lazy man or woman can no more be a successful editor, than they can be good Christians. God never patronizes a lazy Christian, and the world never patronizes a lazy editor. The man or woman who enters the journalistic work expecting to find it a plant which will thrive in a soil of indolence will be grandly disappointed. But to the woman who comes to the work bringing all her talents, her heart and her persistence, success is inevitable. In the newspaper work, especially is that remark of Sir Joshua Reynolds applicable, "If one have great talents, industry will improve them; if you have but moderate abilities, industry will supply the deficiency." The mediocre capacity may be enlarged and made effective by brave resolve and persistent effort. The extreme patience of Woman in most trying circumstances is another thing in her favor. I have known a woman to see

A WHOLE FORM PIED,[26]

when she knew it meant an all-night's hard work, after a day of exhaustive labor, and yet she did not swear about it! If there is a printer in the house, I'll venture ten to one, he could not produce a like prodigy among our male members of the press gang.

The city journalist who has only his special line of work for which he is particularly adapted cannot appreciate, perhaps, the idea that I wish to advance, that Woman is particularly suited to the work of journalism, because of her natural ability to "keep several irons in the fire." I have known a woman to cast a roller while she was cooking her dinner. There is Mrs. Swisshelm; she "knows how it is herself." Women can "set type," read proof, work press if necessary, — and I assure the country journalist finds it necessary to do all these sometimes, especially when the "jour,"[27] is "on a spree," which, alas, is of too frequent occurrence. Were it not for the seeming egotism of the recital, I could give you some distressing accounts of the dilemmas one often finds herself in, in the country printing office, but Woman glories in meeting difficulties and overcoming them.

The most important part of the business in the country newspaper is

CLOSE COLLECTIONS,

and women make splendid collectors generally. I know a woman to collect $600 worth of newspaper debts after her husband had given them up as a dead loss, and one incorrigible old fellow, who was never known before to pay an honest debt, averred that that woman would talk money out of the side of the house.

I am told that women are not as thorough on details as men are. Well, let a woman educated as a reporter, walk beside the male reporter, and she will see twice as much in a walk down street as he will, and can draw just as largely upon her imagination too in reporting it. She therefore don't have to tell any untruths in order to make a matter sensational. As for the girls employed in our office, I find them as efficient as men, and much more reliable, for they never get on a spree!

WOMEN WILL PURIFY NEWSPAPER LITERATURE.

You have heard elaborate and polished discussion upon "the effect of literature upon crime," therefore I will not dwell upon that thought. But a Boston journal a few years ago was horribly shocked at some articles in the *Revolution,* and in holy horror the wise editor penned a half-column editorial, in which he exclaimed that women never entered into journalism but they felt called upon to give expression to ideas upon subjects that had better be discussed in a more private manner. Now, I never saw an article in any woman's journal, not even the most outspoken, that could equal in filthiness any one of the accounts of the recent scandal in high life.[28] The *Revolution* was, and the WOMAN'S JOURNAL is, certainly as dignified a type of journalism as can be found in this country or any other. No obscure, corrupting advertisements appear in their columns, while the disgusting, nauseating filth which too many male journalists seem to take especial delight in serving up to their patrons is rigidly excluded from all journals with which I am acquainted in this country that are under the control of women.

THE SUCCESSFUL COUNTRY PUBLISHER

must have fine executive as well as financial ability, indomitable energy and perseverance, large hope, suavity, and benevolence. The first four are required to make all ends meet, and to insure promptness in the business, which is the very core of success; large hope, to give pluck and courage when the pathway is shaded pecuniarily, as it too often is; and a large fund of benevolence and suavity for the country customer who "just drops in" to talk a whole precious hour on the price of hay or wood, or the crops, or the improvement of stock, that you shall enter so heartily into his spirit that he shall never suspect that you are trembling in your slippers at the sight of the "devil"[29] grinning a request for copy.

The newspaper should be the family educator, and Woman's tact and Woman's heart is much needed in that line. We need more heart in journalism. Remember I am speaking now from my own standpoint as a country journalist. I don't suppose any one looks for much of that article, called heart, in a city newspaper. I read some weeks ago an account of an accidental death in the Exposition[30] in one of your very enterprising dailies, and the deceased was spoken of in much the same flippant manner that you would speak of a hog or a cow that had been run over by some incoming train. If we were to judge the city by its newspapers, we should conclude that all affection and feeling, or even respect, for the dead, were forgotten in the whizz and whirr of business. When

OBITUARIES

cost twenty cents a line, they are not apt to carry much originality or tenderness with them. But the country journalist, to be successful, must enter into the feelings of those about him. There you see again Woman's adaptability. Suppose you were occupying that position, my sisters, and one morning the dear friend who used to go to school with you writes you a pitiful note, wet with her tears, saying that little Jamie, or Annie, or Dick, has gone out from her home, never more to return, with a request that you will tell it tenderly to her friends. As you sit down to pen it, the thread of sympathy that can only be awakened by experience is touched. Your mother heart goes down into the valleys of the bitter past, and resurrects the dead lilies, and the few tender lines you pen about the little dead darling will bear the impress of your own grief when you laid just another such a treasure under the daisies, and the delicate dew of sympathy will not only comfort the just bereaved mother's heart, but hundreds of other mother hearts will take up the refrain, and receive consolation through it. I find that the country journal that fills such a place in the family soon has the heartstrings of a community woven about it to such a degree that one would almost as soon sacrifice the midday meal as to do without that paper. Said a subscriber to the editor of such an one, "I file all your papers, and you can't think what a comfort it is to look them over. I find a faithful epitome of our little city. Here a tender obituary which one cannot read without tears, there a marriage notice in which we can almost hear the wedding bells. I can't help but think what a comfort it will be to the children to look these papers over in after years, and see how we of this generation lived."

THE TRUE JOURNALIST

occupies in the public affections a much more enviable position than even the physician or the minister of the Gospel, for the influences of the latter are, at best, felt only in a small circle, while a live newspaper speaks to the hearts of thousands. There is just as much difference in journalists as there is in preachers. You can very quickly tell the minister who preaches for money from the one who preaches because his great love for humanity and the Master compels his utterance. The world is full of hungry hearts, and the journalist who meets their demands will never lack for work to do. Journalists, like poets, are born, not made. I know two men in the country profession who perhaps have learned this art as well as a woman could. I refer to the late lamented

A. P. Richardson,[31] of McGregor, Ia., the most popular country journalist in the Northwest, and my friend Colfax,[32] of South Bend. There was hardly a man, woman, or child in Iowa who did not know and love the former, while the latter had the happy faculty of so entering into everybody's joys and sorrows that the heartstrings of the people of Northern Indiana are so woven about him that any tide of success or wave of adversity that touches him touches also the whole public heart of that community. Now, I believe there are many women in America who possess this faculty to a happy extent.

We often point to Mr. Colfax, too, and say there are not many men who could start a paper in a country village as South Bend was thirty years ago, upon $800, and clear a debt of $1500 from it in less than three years; but I have the audacity to say, my friends, that I believe there are

PLENTY OF WOMEN

who could do it. If you doubt this, look over the circle of your acquaintance, and see the women who are, every day of their lives, by various contrivances, succeeding in making one dollar do the work of five. Eight years ago my husband and I commenced with $600. To-day we have an office worth $6000, but that $6000 represents many days and nights of persistent toil at the case, in the editorial chair, and sometimes at the press. To help out I have set type all night after working at other branches of the business all day, and I am certain my husband, capable and industrious as he is, would not have been where he is to-day without my aid.

There is as much difference in journalists as in other folks. For instance, although we "guns of smaller calibre" may do the general work and superintending of an office, there are few women, perhaps, who could evince such striking originality as my friend Mrs. Swisshelm, or as Mrs. Stanton, Miss Anthony, or Julia Ward Howe, or Mary Livermore, or Mrs. Soule,[33] so striking that every newspaper in the country is glad to copy their original utterances, but notwithstanding all this many a woman can make herself necessary in a community as a journalist. We can't all be great women or men, but we can dignify the humbler places by doing our work well.

I am often asked: "Does not your professional work

INTERFERE WITH FAMILY DUTIES?"

Well, at the risk of seeming egotistical, I will just tell you how I manage it. I believe the care of our households is very much overdone. For three years of our early married life, when we were sorely cramped for means, I did my own housework, took care of my baby, and filled the positions of local editor and a compositor at the case. My boy is just as happy and healthy for having been much of the time thrown upon his own resources and learning to amuse himself, much more finely developed than if I had spent that precious three years' time in holding and rocking him, and dosing him with Godfrey's Cordial and Mrs. Winslow's Soothing Syrup. I certainly am pecuniarily much better off, and generally much happier, than if I had spent that three years of my life in making frizzles and furbelows to dress him. He is just as apt to be President of the United States for aught I know. The business is "catching" in our family, for the youngest four year old has commenced as carrier on our street, and our little daughter is anxiously looking forward to the day when she shall be an editor.[34]

It is this contact with the rough edges of life that sharpens the intellect, and this accounts for the fact that our great men and women spring from adverse conditions in life. They are the people that, like mullein stocks, will grow in any soil.

Now I do not contend that every woman can be a successful journalist any more than every woman can be a successful physician, or lawyer, or dentist. There is as much difference in women as there is in other folks; but I do believe there is many a fine journalist to-day pining in our millinery and dressmaking shops, and over the wash-tub and ironing-board. I have tried all these branches. I was a miserable failure in all of them, but pecuniarily at least, I have been successful in my present line of business. I love my business dearly—well enough to work sixteen hours of the twenty-four at it, and the work never seems a burden, while the others "were too grievous to be borne." And why should we not choose the occupation we love, so that labor shall be sweet, and we be not driven from morn till night "like galley slaves" to our tasks?

There is less opposition to encounter in this business than most any other of the professions so largely occupied by men. I can only account for this from the fact that the men in this profession are usually the large-hearted, most liberal and unselfish men in the world. There is no other class of men who do so much work for charity, or who are so ready to encourage real merit. I sometimes, when I look over my own experience, feel as if they were even willing to encourage some that were not so real. The Chicago *Times,* and *Inter-Ocean,* and *Tribune* have laid me under many obligations for journalistic courtesies, while the members of our Press Association of Northern Indiana are like a lot of great good-natured brothers, and though now and then I am impaled on the point of their pens, it is always so gently and good-naturedly done that I'm never seriously hurt.

THE EDUCATION FOR THE WORK,

for one who has the adaptablity, is not so slow as in many other professions, while it is an endless progression. You move with the world in newspaper life. A woman with fair literary ability and business tact can learn the business in from three to four years, while the most studious can be but imperfect in many other professions in from four to five years. The country, especially, needs more women journalists. We need more journals to work for the development of our resources, and for all reforms. Woman has hungered and thirsted for a larger field of action until the clock of time has pealed to her four o'clock in the afternoon of the nineteenth century, but it is vain to wait, my sisters, for man's hand to open the door, and press the sweet chalice to your lips. She who would be free, herself must strike the blow! Liberty never descends to any people; they must raise themselves to liberty. I believe with a few hundred women journalists in this country ready to strike for the right I would be willing to risk the elevation, prosperity, happiness, and final emancipation of American women, emancipation from all folly, yea, in the broadest sense of the word.

13

Emma Molloy's Address on Temperance and Woman Suffrage,
American Woman Suffrage Association,
New York, November 17, 1875
Woman's Journal, Dec. 4, 1875, p. 386–87

*This address to a convention of the American Woman Suffrage Asso-
ciation is a reasonably brief example of Emma Molloy's dramatic lecturing
style. It is full of passionate belief in the need for female suffrage and political action in order to accomplish moral reforms such as temperance. The speech
was delivered a few months after her fateful remarks to the Indiana WCTU,
in which she alienated most of the members by saying that prayer alone was
not effective in accomplishing change. She was a delegate of the Woman
Suffrage Association of Indiana.*

I am asked to say something about the status of the Suffrage question in Indiana. The temperance movement which has, for a year and
a half past, been moving over the State like a storm, has proven like
the shock of a galvanic battery to a corpse, only the new life of the
Suffrage movement is not simulated. The shaking of the dry bones has
really raised us up a grand army of earnest men and women who know
in their souls that this temperance battle will never be fought successfully until Woman's influence is felt at the ballot-box. I am not here to
give you a history of that grand battle of the "crusade," in the storm
and shock of which Woman stood like the solid rock, but only to give
some of the grand results. Through the stern lessons of those days,
Woman learned how puny was the hand that held no ballot. When
sixteen thousand of the best and purest women of the city of Chicago
presented their petition to the Mayor and Common Council,[35] asking
the enforcement of the Sunday law, not that the saloons of that city be
closed every day, but only on the Sabbath, you remember the mob that
assailed them upon the street with a flood of obscenity and profanity
that was enough to have made Billingsgate shudder; and how the cowardly police, who were the but too-willing tools of the rum element of
that city, utterly refused to protect them. They were breaking no law
in thus appealing. Have we not always been taught that the right of

petition was the sacred right of every American citizen? And why, when a few weeks before, 12,000 working men had presented their petitions, asking the protection of that same Common Council, had they been received with such marked respect, and these 16,000 intelligent and cultured women with such marked disrespect. Let Mayor Colvin answer for himself. I shall always thank him for his frankness to those ladies, for this sentence rankles yet in the hearts of the women of the Northwest, "Ladies, you have no power to help lift me into office again. I was elected with *this one thing* expressly in view, and I shall obey the behests of my constituency and sign that ordinance to-morrow morning, *though a million women were appealing to me.*" And then and there, not only the women of Chicago, but every thoughtful woman in the Northwest took this lesson home to her heart: "Without the sting of the ballot we are but drones in the great hive of human endeavor."

But the women of the West have learned another lesson in this their period of development; that there is something for the wives and mothers to do in this grand age besides sit and wring their hands in an agony over the slaughter of the innocents. Long enough has Woman hungered and thirsted for justice and liberty, and now, as the great clock of time is striking to her four o'clock in this afternoon of the nineteenth century, at last she has turned upon her pursuers, and is demanding redress. The cry from the white lips of thousands of mothers to-day, is reformation, or revolution, which; and in this Centennial year our brothers are gently reminded that the same patriot blood flows in our veins that pitched King George's tea into Boston harbor, and blood will tell."

(Mrs. Malloy here gave some apt illustrations, which excited some mirth, but which space forbids our giving entire, and closed by saying:)

True, to some the morning dawn of this movement may seem yet far distant, but, as when one down in a well may see stars that never appear to the eyes of these standing out on the open plains of life; so, to the women who have been down in the deep abyss of sorrow, and for many years looking through tears for the first dawn of hope, appears already the star of the East.

The great world may scoff at this movement, but you remember that it was only a very few years ago that Mr. Sumner[36] said that "Liberty was national and slavery was sectional," and all the world but Massachusetts laughed; for slavery sat enthroned in power, clanking the chains of the poor black man, and declaring that her power could not be broken without destroying the Government, and that finally her sceptre "should be borne even unto Bunker Hill." And I remember how the little devoted band, who were the advance guards of liberty, struggled over the desert, following the star of freedom, as a cloud by day and a pillar of fire by night, over deserts and darkness and tribulation, until at last it stood over the South-land, and told to the world that four millions of people were born into a newer and higher life. So again is heard the tocsin of the life guards of the nation, ringing from shore to shore, echoing from the crags of the Alleghenies to the snow-capped peaks of the Sierra Nevadas, telling us of a new star that has dawned, which shall by and by, like a diamond blazing in the dark, burn above our National capitol, proclaiming the emancipation of Woman. The song upon the lips of the world to-day is

> "There's a fount about to stream,
> There's a light about to beam,
> There's a warmth about to glow,
> There's a flower about to blow,
> There's a midnight darkness
>   Changing into gray;
> Men of thought and men of action
>   Clear the way!"

14
Article by Emma Molloy,
Good Templars' Watchword, London, England, October 9, 1878

Emma Molloy's extensive work with American temperance organiza-
tions led to an opportunity for a lecture tour of England in the fall of 1878.
Her presence drew much interest in the temperance community. That the
British Isles were ready for her message is evident from the fact that upon
leaving for America in December, she had to cancel many engagements. Just
two years later, another American temperance speaker, Richard T. Booth,
would spark a powerful and lengthy renewal of the temperance movement.[37]

Most accounts of her lectures and sermons in England are paraphrased,
fragmentary, or extremely long. This article introduced her to the thousands
of readers of the Good Templars' Watchword, *as an American represen-*
tative of progressive, grass-roots temperance. There are some factual errors
in her article (see Notes).

THE BLUE RIBBON BRIGADE.
NEW WAR ON ALCOHOL.
BY SISTER EMMA MOLLOY.

Mrs. Whitney,[38] in one of her works, says "We can only successfully influence *our nexts* in this world, that is those nearest to us, in
thought, feeling and habit," and this has been thoroughly exemplified
in the great Temperance movement now sweeping like a tidal wave over
America, lifting the victims of drink by the thousand upon the high
ground of total abstinence and purity.

The new hope awakened by this movement is that it is no longer
the battle of the philanthropist alone; it has assumed the phase of a
rebellion, a battle for liberty. It bands together in a warfare against drink
those who have been scarred and blighted by it, men who have fairly
rebelled against its thraldom. It originated in this way. In the town of
Bangor, Maine, lived a man[39] who for years had been a slave to drink.
Of sociable, genial temperament, fond of his fellows, he found his reso-
lutions to reform swept to the winds again and again by the invitations
of his old companions, aided by the importunate demands of appetite;

so he resolved to invite his old friends to unite with him in an effort to break away from the bondage that was day by day becoming more and more intolerable. He published a card in the paper inviting all drinking men who desired to quit drink to meet him in a certain hall. Quite a number of his old companions, attracted by the novelty of the request, met him; they reviewed their past lives, and solemnly pledged themselves "for our own sake and the good of the world in which we live, God helping us, to abstain from all intoxicating drink, and to use all our efforts to persuade others to abstain." This was the beginning of the first "Reform Club." The public meetings were addressed by these men, not with studied oratory, but telling the sad stories of their lives in a straightforward, simple, but pathetic manner, which immediately took hold of the public heart. Through their influence hundreds of the patrons of the public-houses were reformed, and enlisted in the ranks of total abstainers. From this Bro. Osgood was called from town to town to organise these Reform Clubs, the badge of which was a little blue ribbon tied conspicuously in the button-hole of the coat or vest, and worn everywhere. It is wonderful how the "little badge of blue" preached as it went. It spread like an epidemic. In many towns in Maine hundreds donned the blue ribbon, with all it implied, and God's blessing went with it.

About this time Frank Murphy,[40] of Portland, Maine, a saloon keeper, one of the representatives of the Emerald Isle, was arrested for accidentally killing a man while intoxicated. The murdered man was making some trouble in Murphy's establishment, and in the endeavour to eject him, being as intoxicated as the proprietor, he slipped from Murphy's grasp, fell down the stairs, and broke his neck.

While lying in gaol, awaiting trial, Murphy was visited by Cyrus Sturtevigant,[41] one of God's own dear messengers who, in the peculiarly tender manner in which he has led so many to Christ, appealed to the manhood of the prisoner. His heart was touched, and the visits of Brother Sturtevigant finally resulted in Murphy's conversion. When he was finally acquitted he was immediately taken into the Osgood Club, donned the blue ribbon, and began work. Probably no man in America has pledged so many drinking men as Francis Murphy. Earnest and eloquent upon the platform, possessed of wonderful magnetic power, thousands flock everywhere to hear him, and are converted. Liquor dealers by the score have joined him, and the whole of New England was set ablaze by Osgood and Murphy with their lieutenants, for as fast as men were pledged they were brought upon the platform, and made to publicly tell their story, and commissioned to go out and help to spread the gospel of total abstinence. About this time Dr. Reynolds,[42] of Maine, was pledged. With the American characteristic which makes every man desire to become a leader, he adopted the red ribbon, his pledge, however, not very materially differing from the Osgood and Murphy pledge. Dr. Reynolds has done a good work through New England and the West, but the blue is stil the predominant colour.

This is a brief history of the rise of the new movement, which, crowned with unparalleled success, has probably enlisted more people than any movement ever inaugurated in America. The real secret of the success of the work is that it takes hold of all the finer feelings of the man. It directly appeals to his honor and manhood; it makes him feel that the public expect something of him; he feels the affectionate support of those who are stronger than himself, and a responsibility for the weaker ones. In the club-room he has the social pleasure which he formerly enjoyed in the public-house, stripped of its pernicious influences; and, best of all, underlying the whole fabric is the sustaining power of Christ.

The Temperance Reform Club is non-sectarian, never meddling with a man's peculiar religious views. We have enrolled men of all shades of religious belief; we have Catholics and Protestants, all relying on God for help, but keeping the question of total abstinence above all others.

This, dear *Watchword*, is the work in which your humble correspondent has been engaged for the past three years, and which I come to bring to England. It has already been introduced with marvellous success by Bro. William Noble, in London, aided by Bro. Captain De Carteret,[43] both of them Reformed men. I believe it is *the* movement for the working men of England. Every Good Templar ought to be interested in it, because any and every instrumentality which advances the sobriety of the people strengthens our hands. Our mission is to "reclaim the fallen and keep others from falling."

We who were identified with the great crusade, or Whiskey War, in America, can but feel that this new movement is the answer to the thousands of prayers that ascended from broken-hearted women, that God's arm might be made bare, that the Holy Spirit would guide and direct the work, and a new era be inaugurated in the history of the Temperance Reform. As nearly as can be estimated, more than a million men have already been redeemed through this instrumentality, and a national organisation is already contemplated. I trust the seed may be as industriously planted in Great Britain this winter, and that we may have the co-operation of all earnest Temperance men and women in pushing the good work forward.

15
Emma Molloy's Address and Poem for Decoration Day
South Bend Daily Tribune, May 31, 1878

During her years of constant traveling on the "temperance track," as she called it, Emma Molloy sometimes had a chance to return home for a brief rest. In May, 1878, she spoke at the South Bend City Cemetery.

Memory is playing strange pranks with me to-day and the faces of many of these fallen comrades are strangely intermingled with many familiar faces before me. I remember how some who are here, waited through long weary days which never came, and who mourn over graves far away in the sunny south, over whom, perchance, no friendly hand may scatter flowers to-day. I remember that there are those among us who ought to be as dear to us as is the memory of those fallen braves, because they have *lived* through days and nights of anguish and loneliness known only to them and to God, for
"Heroes there are, never showing the mark,
of the thrust in the heart or the blow in the dark."
and, brothers, I am grateful to you for the honor you have shown me in thus permitting me to add my mite to the glorious words which have here been spoken in memory of these fallen braves, many of whom were my schoolmates and personal friends. It is like a weird, wild dream; the enlistment, the muster, the parting with kindred and friends, the drill, the march; the battles when we stayed at home and watched the papers for the names of the missing and wounded; the long nights and days of suspense; the imprisonment of some whose tales of suffering have made Libby and Andersonville[44] seem like ghostly nightmares— oh, would we could under the lilies and roses bury all that is sad, and think of them only as glorified. Yet our pain is not unmingled with pride to remember that their valor helped to preserve the priceless gem of constitutional law and social order which our fathers died to establish; and if we have a united country, if we enjoy the blessing of civil and religious liberty, it is due to our soldier brothers who stood like a wall of fire between us and destruction. Then,

Come with music loving and tender,
    Come with footsteps solemn and slow,
Come with banners homage to render
    To our brave heroes lying so low.

These were our boys that we loved in the Maytime,
    Ere the frosts of life's winter had silvered our hair;
These were our brothers, and in the old playtime
    Twined for us garlands of flowers so fair.

Why should we not bring the blossoming roses,
    Lilacs, and lilies, and rosemary too,
Marking the mounds where calmly reposes
    Our patriot heroes who honored the Blue.

'Tis said that flowers are God's love letters
    Writ yearly to tell us how by and by
We shall break away from these earthly fetters
    And blossom in beauty with Him on high.

Buried each year in the earth's brown bosom,
    Called in the spring by his loving breath
Forth in new beauty, they teach this lesson
    To sorrowing hearts, *There is no death.*

That by and by we too shall be sleeping
    With friend and with lover under the sod,
But 'tis only the husk earth holds in her keeping,
    While the souls are abloom in the garden of God.

Oh, then could we find a language more tender,
    To tell of our loving for these loyal ones,
The yearnings of maiden for lover or brother,
    Of wife for the husband or mothers for sons?

Speak to them, roses and lilies and pansies,
    Lilacs and myrtle and sweet mignonette,
Carry back on your fragrance our loving remembrance,
    Oh, tell them we miss them and mourn for them yet;

That we've never forgotten their loving devotion,
    That your faces this day with our tears have been wet;
That we've spoken each name with tenderest emotion,
    And cherish their memory with loving regret.

Do souls e'er reply up in Heaven, I wonder,
    To remembrances tender of lonely hearts here?
Can time or space or the grave ever sunder
    The lives that have thrilled in such sympathy here?

Oh, may not some strain of our music ascending
    Rend the blue vaults of bliss where they walk now in white?
May no answering chords on our souls swift descending
    Cheer us on in our battles for God and the Right?

Then trusting they see from some hillside in glory
    The love-tokens we lay o'er their mouldering dust,
We will come year by year in song and in story
    To tell how our heroes were true to their trust.

O green be the turf forever above them.
    And green be their memory forever and aye;
We may pass from the earth who mourn them and love them,
    But this nation will not let their names fade away.

And yearly she'll bring the blossoming roses
    Lilacs and myrtle, the bay and the yew,
Marking these mounds where calmly reposes
    Our patriot-heroes who honored the Blue.

16

Emma Molloy's Address to the Kansas WCTU Convention,
Leavenworth, Kansas, October 21, 1884
Kansas Commoner, Leavenworth, October 25, 1884

*Vivid, well-structured, reasoned argument had long been a strength
of Emma Molloy's public speaking. This address comes from the 1884 Presidential campaign, in which Emma Molloy as editor of the* Morning and
Day of Reform *threw all her efforts behind former Kansas Governor John
P. St. John's campaign for President on the Prohibitionist ticket. It reveals
her thinking and her strategies in taking this "losing" political position.
Speaking at an evening meeting at the Baptist church in Leavenworth,
according to the newspaper she was "listened to throughout with great and
frequent applause."*

I come before my old friends in Leavenworth under a pressure
to-night which I cannot describe. I am aware as I stand before you I
am to address people who honestly differ with me in the issues now
before us. For the first time in the ten years that I have been before the
public I have found my old co-workers dropping away from me; I have
met averted looks from those whose faces have heretofore brightened
at my coming. I have had good men and good women say "I know you
are right but the time has not yet come! for this movement."

Friends, the time is coming when we shall again see eye to eye;
when the pressure of public sentiment will right the parties that are
toiling, and the new revolution will be a success. It will not matter in
that glad day what becomes of you and me if only the right over the
wrong prevails. I beg you to listen to me candidly, and prayerfully remember it is an honest heart, pleading the case of the home against
the saloon to-night.

There are in the United States three classes carrying on a triangular fight over the dram-shop system of the country.

The first claim that it is a legitimate and respectable business, and
that it ought to be unrestricted as any other business!

The second claim that it is an evil business and ought to be con-
trolled, but declare that you cannot do anything about it!

The third claim that it is a crying sin and evil upon which there can be no compromise; and that the drunkard making system must be destroyed root and branch. That it is an enemy to this government; an enemy to law and civilization, and that there is no reason under the heavens why any honest man should by his vote sustain a system that stimulates riots in our great cities, demoralizes society; laughs at the corruption of the ballot box; ruins the peace and prosperity of the home, and makes the protection of life, liberty and the pursuit of happiness, impossible!

The whole issue involved is simply a question of fact. If the liquor traffic is a blessing every patriotic American, every man who loves his country owes it to his citizenship, to his own sense of honor to stand by the traffic, to work for it, talk for it, vote for it! If you are a praying man get down on your knees and pray for it. If you believe that the White Elephant is a help to the morals of the people of Leavenworth you are a humbug if you don't preach for it, and lend to it the grace of your presence.

If the reverse is true, if the liquor traffic is a curse to the community, if it is a stream of corruption in politics, if it is the plague-spot on the heart of the nation, if it is a disease that is threatening our National life, and you dare to stand "Trembling cowering in presence of this grievous wrong, when with one bold stroke these groaning millions might be free; and that one stroke so just, so nobly good, so level with the happiness of man that all the angels may applaud the deed." And should you refuse to strike the blow, then I say you are unworthy the name of American free men. This government is the child of that morality, that theory of religious liberty, that system of governmental life which was taught by the men who settled and developed the colonies, who gave us our Declaration of Independence, and who framed the constitution guaranteeing the protection of life, liberty and the pursuit of happiness, and who always remembered their duty to Almighty God. In other words this government is the outgrowth of the homes, it is built from the bottom not from the top. The home organizes, their families assemble and you have the village; then the township, then the county, then the state; and the nation is the aggregation of all these. What the home is then will determine what the nation will be in a government like ours. Will you show me in all the history of the world the record of a single commercial nation, a Sabbath breaking, liquor-drinking, God-defying people, that has maintained a government of the people, for the people and by the people for a single century? The great French Statesman Montulamberc[4] says: "Without a Sabbath, no worship; without worship, no religion; without religion no permanent freedom."

Now the great question of the hour in America is not the Chinese question; not the tariff question; not the protection of the sheep of the country, but it is a question of what we shall do with the liquor traffic? Whether we shall arise in our might and overthrow this evil thing that a few years ago was a suppliant at the foot of the throne, and next the power behind the throne, and now the power upon the throne. The question of what this government will do with the liquor traffic is not one that can be settled with a wave of the hand and a sneering laugh! It will not down! It is a question that has got to be heard and settled and settled right no matter which party goes up or which party goes down. The liquor traffic of the nation is on trial for its life. The home is pressing the indictment, and there isn't money or political power enough in all the whole business to prevent the final verdict of the people. You should weigh honestly every argument on both sides and make up your verdict in accordance with the facts, remembering that as James G. Blaine says: "The liberty of the individual ceases where the rights of society begins."

The Democratic party claim to have the clearest conception of the nature of prohibition. They understand its properties to be, like leaven and so they want to get it entirely out of the party; there is no uncertain sound in their utterance. They declare themselves in favor of blotting out all sumptuary laws that vex the citizen and interfere with individual liberty. The Democratic party as a party line up on the side of the saloon and we know exactly where to find it in this battle.

The Republicans are trying to keep Prohibition in the party, but to prevent its spread and keep it under control. This question is precisely like the old Whig party to that of the anti-slavery movement of its time. When the fact became clearly known to the anti-slavery men and women that the Whig party was powerless in the hands of the pro-slavery party they withdrew from it and the party died.

The Republican party arose from its ruins with anti-slavery in its platform, and in ten years slavery died. Never till the Republican party dies, is buried, and rises again in newness of life and in a glorified body will it help to strangle the rum power. It is just as good a time for that burial in this year of grace 1884 as ever we will have in the history of the Nation. There are no great issues before the people except this abolition of the drink tariff, the murder-manufacturers and the crime breeders!

Oh! yes says my Republican friend, "There is the great tariff question!" But every sensible man before me tonight knows that this is but a man of straw. The principles upon which the tariff duties are adjusted were determined upon in the last generation and these principles are accepted by the people. The changes in the schedule that are from time to time made according to these principles and the exigencies of business, are arranged by private conference and not by public meetings. It will not make a particle of difference in the tariff, whoever is elected President. It is also immaterial to me whether a President goes into power who is in favor of abolishing all laws restricting the liquor traffic, or the one who is in favor of making the tax a permanent source of revenue.

Dear friends, there is a grand army that are going to stand up and be counted for principle, and in four years from now the ministers and lawyers, and teachers and doctors who vote as they pray will be respected as much at least as the average saloon keeper. A leading American was asked in Boston "Would you plunge the colonies in war for a few pence on a pound of tea?"

The answer was it is not the amount of tax, but the accursed principle upon which parliament bases the claim of right to levy any tax that we are fighting. It was fought out on that line and King George lost the brightest jewel in his crown! Friends there is a little of the old blood left yet in American (s) that pitched King George's tea into the Boston Harbor, and blood will tell! It cannot always be held down. For a time his unjust commands were obeyed, but there came the time when the swelling tide of resistance could no longer be stayed, and the just indignation of the people hurled him from his throne of power into the dungeon which his crimes so richly merited.

So the liquor power of this nation has cried to the political parties keep the people back, and they have striven to obey but to-day the swelling tide of resistance cannot longer be stayed. The people cannot be kept back, and on the 9th of November a million voters will express their verdict at the ballot box.

From the day the temperance reform began in this country, there has been no concealment of its objects and purposes. Its advocates have asserted from every platform in this land that their object is to destroy the drunkard making system. No compromise measure will satisfy. Compromise upon a question of principle is always a victory for the devil. If you know that you are right, if your conscience and reason tells you that you are right, and for the sake of a temporary peace you concede to the side that you know is wrong, you are certain to lose ground, and you will find that eventually you must retrace the steps you have taken before you can settle the matter.

Reviewing the history of the struggle for the abolition of slavery the lecturess said that the shedding of blood taught the American people that a great question is never settled until it is settled right.

The calm dispassionate purpose of the temperance element of this country is to have this question between the home and the saloon settled, and settled right. Wendell Phillips[46] once said the reason why the liquor men always succeed is because they know exactly what they want and are determined to have it; when the temperance men know exactly what they want and are determined to have it we shall succeed and not till then.

Well in this year of grace 1884 we have found out exactly what we want, and are not going to stop until we get it. The purpose of the Home Protection Party[47] is to bury the liquor business of the country in the same way the old Welsh woman said she would bury the devil, with face down so that if he should ever come to life the more he dug the deeper he would get.

We are sorry the Republican party in the nation wouldn't lend a hand, but we are going to get the grave ready and when the funeral comes off there will be plenty of mourners from the Republican party.

"But they tell me you cannot elect your candidate!" Oh! no, not this year. We are aware that it is some time after a declaration of war before the armies are brought into final conflict. There is the previous arousement, the useful drill of the camp of instruction before the final combat. For 16 years the old parties have said keep this question out of politics. Wait until the people are educated in prohibition sentiment! Why if you wait till an army drills itself, it will be a long time before it is up in military tactics. We are organized to educate the people. We will not stop when the election is over in November. The old parties will have decided whether the ins shall stay in, or the outs shall go in; but in the press, the pulpit; on the rostrum, before the great court of public opinion we shall go on preparing the case against the criminal. We shall educate the masses to know that no man throws away his vote, when it is an honestly planted as opposed to a great wrong in the nation.

Friends this is not a question simply of the present hour which we have come to settle. It is a question that reaches down into the century; it is touching the future of this nation. The birth of this new party is simply the herald of that better day that is coming when men shall scorn to be clods; when rising to the grand civilization which our constitution guarantees, the voters of America shall issue a new Declaration of Independence.

At the battle of Chicamauga, brave old Gen. Steadman[48] saw one of his regiments wavering under the terrible fire of the enemy and beginning to retreat, he seized the flag and shouted: "You can go to the rear but you shall not take this flag with you."

So there may be some of our old friends who will break ranks under the enemy's fire and they may go to the rear, but they can't take the flag with them. There are plenty of brave hands to hold aloft the white banner of prohibition and keep it in the front of the battle till the victory is won. It is coming friends.

"Oh aid the dawning tongue and pen,
    Aid it hopes of honest men,
Aid it papers, aid it type
    Aid it for the hour is ripe,
And our earnest must not slacken into play.
Men of thought and men of action clear the way."

17

Excerpts from Emma Molloy's Self-Defense,
Springfield Express, May 14, 1886

*During the time of the preliminary hearing into the murder of Sarah
Graham, George Graham, egged on by a scandal-hungry press, penned state-
ments from his prison cell that cast doubt on Emma's moral character. At the
end of April, shortly after Graham was lynched by an angry mob, a booklet
recounting the entire matter was published by a Springfield newspaper.*

*No rebuttal had yet come from Emma herself. Finally, on May 14,
1886, the* Springfield Express *and other newspapers carried her long, detailed letter, in which she rebutted, point by point, the charges made against
her by Graham and others.*

*Due to the extreme length and detail of the letter, just the first part,
containing her general remarks, is excerpted here. It gives a sense of Emma's
state of mind in this crisis. Her complaints about exploitation by the press
resonate loudly today.*

Mrs. Molloy's Statement
Springfield, Mo., May 10, 1886

To the Public:

For several weeks my friends all over the United States have been
imploring me for the refutation of the slanderous charges made by
George E. Graham in his 'statement,' which was launched upon the
world while we were in the midst of a preliminary examination, under
charges of a crime which was committed when I was three hundred
miles away, and of which I had not the slightest knowledge until I read
it in the newspapers. Did I believe that Cora Lee Graham was capable
of participation in so horrible an affair, or that she could ever have
connived at, or consented to, or ever known of, and concealed so un-
natural a crime, I should never set pen to paper in her defense in any
way; but I do believe in her innocence, not only of the crime charged
by the courts, but the knowledge that she was an unlawful wife, or of
the slanderous assertions of Graham who in one breath declares her to
be the one woman of all the world to him, and in the next charges her

with criminality such as could only be practiced by the vilest woman...

I am aware that it is impossible in a brief newspaper article to present anything like a lucid history of the connection of Graham with my family. This would require the relation of details and the publishing of correspondence that would fill a volume. I expect, if spared, soon to issue a history of my prison and reform work, which will read like a romance, and will present quite another side of the case than has been given to the public.[49] The world may then perhaps not wonder so much that we were deceived, for the public has been made aware that this man had no ordinary brain.

I know how unwise any lengthy statement would be at this stage of affairs. I fully realize the delicacy of my position, and my only apology for intruding myself upon the public in this defense is, that I owe it to the cause of Christ, which these charges show I foully dishonored were they true; I owe it to my children who, in my public assassination, have suffered untold agony, for it has smitten down their sole protector; to the noble and true friends who have never wavered in their allegiance to me, though to some who have stood closely by me it has been like carrying their own reputations down into the valley and shadow of death; lastly to myself, for I regard my life as a holy trust not to be carelessly thrown away, else it would have been a blessed relief during the past few weeks to have laid aside the weary burden, and sought in the refuge of the grave a relief from the merciless storm of persecution which has been waged against me. It is seldom a human being is called upon to go through such a fire as has been kindled about me.

It takes a lifetime to build character. It is the work of years to establish a good name, and for a woman thrust by life's emergencies into a public position as I have been, it is a battle inch by inch with all the odds against her, and such is the structure of society that the breath of slander from the lips of ever so characterless a man, may in an hour demolish the work of all the years, or at least so impair it that she is forever crippled. I cannot wonder, stranger as I was to the people of Springfield, that the horrible occurrences of the past few months have made the public severe in its denunciations and dealings with me, or that those who were my friends have silently stood aloof waiting to see the outcome, and demanding an explanation and refutation of all the charges made against myself and Cora Lee. I rather marvel at the pure gold of the true and unwavering friendship of the noble men and women, who, knowing so little as they did in the beginning of this trial, of my real inner life, have stood bravely by me in good and evil report To Judge Baker[50] and his dear wife, who have in their courageous defense been so unflinching, I owe a debt of gratitude that all eternity can scarcely repay. To the members of the W.C.T.U. and other lady friends who in the trying scenes in the court room stood like a wall of iron around me while cold, gray eyes steel-bladed were piercing me through, and I was hunted to the death; when it took the courage of their convictions to show me sympathy, and the sneers of the thoughtless rabble, and a sensational press made it a literal crucifixion; I can only say they have proven that our 'legion of the pledge and the cross' is composed of the noblest specimens of womanhood, and have forever given the lie to the oft repeated slander that 'women never stand by women when they are slandered and persecuted.'

To the gentlemen who, like brothers rallied to my rescue, signing my bond because convinced of my innocence of the crime with which I was charged, and to whom I owe a life long debt of gratitude; to those, and to hundreds of loyal friends at whose hearth-stones I have been a welcome guest, and whose letters have come to me like a benediction, it is due that I now, as I wished to do the day following the publication of the slanderous statement of George Graham, positively deny the truth of all...slanderous allegations. I was then met with the argument, 'you must establish the truth of your denial *beyond your mere assertions.* It must be done by affidavit, positively proving your whereabouts on the dates in which he charges the criminal intimacy to have occurred;' and I was silenced, for I remembered that there are no two classes of people whom the world, especially the suspicious part of it, so readily believe a scandal about (than) a minister and a woman, but when the two characters are combined, and a scandal can be concocted sufficiently ingenious for the public to swallow, however nauseating and polluting it may be, it is devoured with an ecstasy of delight. It matters not that hearts may break or lives go out in grief, if but these human vultures of society may fatten upon the slain reputations of others.

18
Essay by Emma Molloy Barrett,
Pacific Christian Advocate, November 23, 1904

Religion, which had always been very important to Emma, for the last twenty years of her life became her main occupation. In this article published less than three years before her death, Emma Molloy Barrett, traveling as an evangelist on the West coast, gives a vivid account of the good deeds of another woman who, like her, sought to be of help.

THE MINISTRY OF LOVE.
Emma M. Barrett, Evangelist.

I wonder if the general traveling public realize what a beautiful thing it is for the railroad company to keep that sweet-faced, gentle matron in the Union Depot at Portland to look after the needs of the old and feeble ones, and to mother friendless girls unused to the ways of a wicked world?

My train was five hours late. I was hastening to fill an appointment, and dismayed to find that I must spend the day in Portland. Too weary to go about the city, I settled myself down in the waiting-room with a book. A score of disgruntled passengers were looking cross and dispirited, or stupid and sleepy. Just then a forlorn old man, pale and feeble, tottered in, and sat down near me. His lips were blue, and his gray locks disheveled. The quick eye of the matron saw that he was in distress. In reply to her kind inquiries, he said: "I am faint, but I can't eat. If I only had something warm to drink it would help me, but I ain't got no appetite for my lunch."

There was an utter weariness in the old face that seemed like a touch of the Master's hand, whispering the "Inasmuch as ye have done it unto the least of these." She kindly said, "There is a place out here where you can get some hot tea. I'll go and show you." He hesitated, and then a pitiful look came into the old eyes as he said, "Yes, ma'am, but I have no money to buy it," and a shiver went through the thinly clad old body.

Without a word, she turned away, was gone a few minutes, and returned with a steaming cup of tea.

"Well, now, ain't that nice!" and he tremblingly undid the frugal lunch, and began to sip the warm tea, and as the color crept into the pale cheeks, his eyes followed her with grateful tenderness.

She now seated herself beside a young girl to whom a gaudily dressed woman was whispering. As the procuress, for such she was, hastily left, Mrs. Niles said:

"What was she saying to you, my child?"

"Why, she asked me if I would not like to go out and see the Fair grounds, and go home with her and have lunch, and she would get me back to the train in time. I told her yes, I would like to go."

The baffled creature stood in the door scowling at the matron, who replied: "My child, don't let any one lure you out of this depot. That woman would never bring you back here." And as her character and object was explained, the young girl with a look of terror on her face, nestled closer to the motherly woman who stood between her and destruction.

The old man had finished his cup of tea, and with a look of sweet content upon his face as she took the cup from the trembling old hands, he said: "God bless you, daughter! It tasted so good, and I feel quite comfortable. I was feelin' a little down-hearted, and like as if I hadn't any friends, but I feel 'most as good as new now."

"All aboard for the train for Ta-co-ma, Se-at-tle, and all points north!" rang out the call through the depot, and I saw her assisting the old man, and caring for the sweet young girl until they were safely seated in the train, and the conductor instructed to look out for them.

Another inrush of passengers, and a half-clothed crowd of children followed a sickly looking woman with a wan little baby in her arms. The mother had no wrap. Her money had given out, and she had nothing to eat. The children were whispering together, and the younger ones were crying. The mother drew the youngest to her, and wiped his face on a soiled handkerchief, saying, "Don't cry, we will get there after awhile." The matron approached and said:

"Where are you going?"

"To Everett, ma'am. Our train was late, and we've missed connection. My husband sent for us, but we didn't have quite money enough, and my children are crying from hunger. I tell 'em we must stand it till we get to papa."

Again the matron went away, and was seen talking with some of the men about the depot. She was telling of the distress of this little family. "Now, boys, you must help me," she said. In a few minutes she had collected enough to buy a substantial basket of lunch, enough to last them to their destination. While they were eating it, one of the men looked in at the door, and beckoning to the matron, he shyly put a golf cape in her hands, saying, "Wife says she can spare that for the poor woman."

Great content was written on her face as she nestled the baby under its warm folds and said, "Oh, how I thank you!"

And so day after day the surging tide of life goes through the depot, and that dear, quiet woman, who seems always to know the right thing to do, like a magician, smoothes the rugged way for the weary, tired feet that have found life's way thorny. This is only a glimpse of her work. I could tell much more would time and space permit; but, reader, will you not send up to God a prayer for the noble woman who day by day lifts the burdens from the weak, the weary and helpless?

BRIEF CHRONOLOGY

1839 Born Emily F. Barrett in South Bend, Indiana, July 17

1841 Death of her mother, Harriett Newton Barrett

1858 Marriage to Louis Pradt and move to Wisconsin

1861 Birth of her daughter Lottie

1863 Birth of her son Allie; death of Lottie

1864 Death of Allie

1867 Return to South Bend, divorce; marriage to Edward Molloy, began work on *South Bend National Union*

1870 Birth of son Franklin; first public lecture on "Woman"

1872 Move to Cortland, NY; then back to Elkhart where Molloys began the *Elkhart Observer*

1874 Beginning of career as temperance lecturer

1876 Started work for Ribbon movement in New England

1878 Lecturing tour of England

1879 Began prohibition amendment work and writing/editing for the *Morning and Day of Reform*

1882 Divorce and move to Elgin, Illinois

1883 Began work with Cherokee Indians in Oklahoma

1884 Move to Washington, Kansas and proprietorship of the *Morning and Day of Reform*

1885 Failure of the *Morning*; move to Springfield, Missouri

1886 Murder case at Springfield and lynching of George Graham; death of Frank Molloy and Emma's near death by drowning

1887 Began evangelistic work on the West Coast

1888 Move to Port Townsend, Washington

1889 Married Morris Barrett

1907 Last revivals; death in California, May 14

EMMA'S FAMILY

Great-Grandparents (paternal)
Thornton Barrett (c. 1730-1806)
Abigail Bowker Barrett (1740-1816)
Jonathan Bosworth, Jr. (c. 1750-c. 1819)
Mary Holt Bosworth (1754-c. 1848)

Grandparents
John Barrett, Sr. (1773-1856)
Susannah Bosworth Barrett (1775-1870)
Joseph Newton (1774-1843)
Susannah Newton (Hackney) (c. 1793-1874)

Parents
William Lovell Barrett (1810-1899)
Harriett Newton Barrett (c. 1813-1841)

Stepmother
Harriett Eaker Barrett (1822-1898)

Siblings
Clement Barrett (1837-1838)
Eliza H. Barrett (1841-1841)

Half-Siblings (children of William L. & Harriett Eaker Barrett)
Zilpha Barrett Hogue (1853-c. 1891)
William E. Barrett (1857-193?)
John C. Barrett (1859-1940)
May Barrett (1863-1943)
Edward Barrett (c. 1865-1887)

Half-Great-Nephew
J. Barrett Guthrie (1922—) (Grandson of John C. Barrett)

Husbands
Louis A. Pradt (c. 1831-18??)
Edward Molloy (1843-1914)

Morris Barrett (1835-1903)
(Also a first cousin: son of her father's brother, John
Barrett, and Clara Cook Barrett)

Children
Lottie Pradt (daughter) (1861 1863)
Allie Pradt (son) (1863-1864)
Franklin Molloy (1870-1886)

Adopted Child
De'Etta ("Etta") Molloy Blakeney (Smith) (1867-1944)
(original name: Mary Frances Pogue)

Daughter of Adopted Child
Emma DeEtta Blakeney Hunsaker (1891-1968)

Granddaughter of Adopted Child
Frances Emma Hunsaker Carter (1915-1992)

Great-Granddaughter of Adopted Child
Jean Carter Hass (1941—)

Stepchild
Clarence F. Barrett (c. 1861-c. 1940)
(son of Morris and Kate Kilpatrick Barrett)

Step-Grandchild
Florence Barrett Coughlan (1896-1983)

Step-Great-Grandchild
Constance Coughlan Moore Barron (1920—)

Foster Children
Cora E. Lee Juel (c. 1860-19??)
Bessie Birekes Thomas (c. 1885-19??)[1]

THE RIBBON WORKERS, 1878

Here is Emma Molloy's story as written by an admiring author of her time. In The Ribbon Workers, *James M. Hiatt presented biographies of several men and women who, like Emma, had been devoting themselves with success to the work of the Ribbon temperance movement.*

Though the following narrative contains some errors of fact (see Notes) as well as many biographical details which cannot be verified, in its portrayal of Emma's work it gives intimate glimpses of some of her important efforts. It is clearly based on Emma's story as she herself told it in her many temperance speeches. It conveys something of the flavor of the passion she brought to her work. And it gives the sources she credited for that passion.

LIFE OF MRS. EMMA MOLLOY
From *The Ribbon Workers* by James M. Hiatt
(J. W. Goodspeed, Chicago, 1878)

CHAPTER I.

HER CHARACTER AS AN ORATOR—HER MOTIVE POWER—WHAT THE DRINK-DEMON DID FOR HER—THE INSPIRATION BORN OF SORROW.

"She hath offered what she had."—MARK'S GOSPEL, Chapter 14, verse 8.

As an effective orator before the masses on the subject of temperance, Mrs. Emma Molloy is undoubtedly the first woman of America. Such is the verdict of the people throughout the Western[1] and the New England States, wherever she has been heard. If, in her own special line, she has a female peer in any other part of the world, the fact is not known on our side of the Atlantic. And, speaking frankly, her performances exhibit a combination of logic and eloquence, which we rarely find among male speakers of the same class. As a close, analytic reasoner, she is a Dr. Russell,[2] while in descriptive power and dramatic effect she is a John B. Gough.[3] In her use of these varied talents she displays the most admirable tact. She first captures the intellect by regular, argumentative approaches. Then, with touching pictures and overwhelming appeals, she carries the heart by storm.

This great little woman, who, as Locke said of Pope,[4] has scarcely body enough to cover mind respectably, is a native Hoosier, having been born and reared in South Bend. Her mother and father were pioneer settlers of Indiana during the period of its infancy. They braved all the dangers and endured all the hardships of frontier life. The mother, with a devotion beautiful as rare, and with a culture which would have made her the idol of the social and literary circle which she left, accompanied her husband to the banks of the St. Joe, beginning her married life in a log cabin. She was a working Christian, and a very efficient teacher, both of religion and of the common branches of learning. She was, therefore, in great demand among the rude frontiersmen as an instructor of youth in letters and of grown folks in morals. It was not long till her cabin-home was required to serve the purposes of a school-room and a mission church, while upon her devolved the double task of teaching "the young idea how to shoot" and the old idea how to behave.

Although thus taxed week-day and Sunday, she was never found wanting in her domestic duties. Strange as it may appear to some, she never complained, but always rejoiced, under the weight of her great responsibilities. In a letter to a friend she once said, "I am glad of the ability to help my husband, and still more glad that the Master has opened to me a field of usefulness to my fellows."

To what extent the present generation of our Western people are indebted to such noble, self-sacrificing women as she was, will never be known till God shall present the account. She taught, not only the children of the white people of her neighborhood, but those of the Indians who still remained in the vicinity.

Being a woman of slight, delicate frame, she fell, in a few years, a victim to the malarious climate, and a glorious martyr in the highest interests of our common humanity, at the early age of twenty-eight years.

After her death her husband broke up house-keeping, and Emma was for eleven years left a motherless waif, boarding around from place to place, and rarely getting to see her father, whose business called him away most of the time. How she hungered and thirsted for a mother's love; how she starved for a mother's sympathy; how she mourned the loss of home; how, after night-fall, she used to walk out under the quiet stars, throw herself upon the ground, and wish that she could drift out of this lonesome, desolate world—none but herself can ever know.

Thus early began that training in sorrow which is now so visible in the melancholy glances of her beautiful gray eye, and which has had so much to do in determining her course of life.

Just what her educational advantages were during her girlhood, I do not know. Nor do I know the number of her school-years. But they must have been few; for before she was out of her teens she was a wife and a mother.[5] It is evident, however, that in some way or other, and at some time or other, her mind has been well informed and thoroughly disciplined. This is no less manifest in her private conversation than it is in her lectures.

We now come to that which inspired her to enter public life, and which constitutes the secret of her remarkable power on the platform.

The drink-demon came into the very sunrise of her married life, and robbed it of its sweetness. That fiend rolled upon her heart a burden which, though she has learned to bear it, has never for one moment ceased to oppress her. All her girlish expectations lie withered at the feet of the monster who slew the first man she ever loved, in the bloom of his manhood.

A tender, motherless child, she came to that husband with a heart brimming over with affection—an affection more to be prized, in these days of convenient marriages, than all the gold in the world. She came, bringing health, and hope, and purity, and fidelity, never dreaming that at the root of her rose tree of happiness, there was a canker-worm feeding upon its sap, and that soon every beautiful blossom would be dead. Upon becoming a wife, she went with her husband to live in Sheboygan. Here, after she had been just three weeks a bride, he was brought to her home one night dead-drunk. She had never before seen a man in that condition, and the leaden-like stupor excited in her the gravest fears. Irresolutely she walked back and forth from the bed on which he lay to the door, hesitating as to whether she should expose her grief and shame by calling in the assistance which she could not but regard as being essential. Finally her fear overcame her pride. She went to one of her nearest neighbors, timidly knocked at the door, called for the lady of the house, and said to her in a tremulous voice—"I believe my husband is dying." The kind-hearted neighbor-woman, with her good man, immediately followed Emma to the bedside of the besotted sleeper, after one look into whose face the motherly little matron turned and folded the young wife in her arms and tenderly exclaimed, "My poor child!" while her spouse, less considerate, if not less sympathetic, calmly remarked, "O, he'll not die to-night. He's only drunk."

Did you ever stand in the sunshine and suddenly feel a thick blackness settle around you? Did you ever have the blood curdle about your heart as if a great iron hand with an iron grip were upon it? So it was with girlish, sensitive Emma at this moment. As her two friends walked out of her door the bright angel of hope went out with them, and cloud-winged despair sat down in the place of that sweet messenger.

Emma threw herself upon the sofa and pressed her cold fingers upon her hot, tearless eyelids. Then she tottered to the door and looked up at the clear, starry sky vainly seeking there one little thread of calmness. When that night settled down upon her she was a joyous child, but after it had rolled its twelve long, heavy hours over her bruised heartstrings, she was a woman, and life was never again the same to her. O, how rapidly the pressure of sorrow matures the soul!

On coming to himself once more, the husband, of course, promised repentance. Meantime he tried to comfort his little wife with the idea that "a fellow's getting tight now and then was so common that, after all, his little spree didn't amount to much." But this, instead of mitigating, intensified her pain, by discovering to her that real humility was not then in his heart.

The mask once thrown off, the descent was swift and terrible. The time eventually came when he was aroused to a sense of his danger, and when he would fain have fled from his merciless pursuer. But it was then too late. The appetite, which there was every reason to believe had been inherited, raged with resistless fury. Deciding that it would be best to break up old associations, he and his wife moved to

Mishawaka, a village about four miles from South Bend. But no improvement in his habits was effected by this change. Being a printer, he was employed by a paper in Mishawaka. In a short time, however, he was discharged on account of drunkenness. Emma then procured a job for him on the *Mail* in Montgomery, Alabama, through two of her cousins, and moved with him to that city, hoping he would there turn over a new leaf. But O, vain hope! In the Sunny South his course was worse than it had ever been at home. It was not long till his ever-growing thirst for liquor consumed all his means and his household goods. Emma now returned to South Bend, Ind. Here and at this time she gave birth to a little girl—Lottie. After somewhat recovering her health and strength she followed her husband to Madison, Wisconsin, in which place she was reduced by his profligacy to the necessity of taking in washing and sewing in order to keep soul and body together.

In the course of time a little boy was added to her family and to the already mountainous load of her cares. Her health now began to fail; and the battle for bread, with a husband who, not only provided nothing, but spent for whisky no small amount of her hard and scanty earnings, was fierce and cruel beyond the comprehension of those who have never had a like experience. O, who can depict the impenetrable gloom, the terrible anguish of this period? And who will wonder that there were moments when her load seemed greater than she could bear—moments in which she felt tempted to comply with the only condition on which her friends proposed to assist her—that she should give up trying to save the poor wreck for whom there appeared to be no hope. But when she would hint this to him there would come in his eyes a hopeless terror, and like a drowning man catching at a straw, he would clutch her to his heart in a wild, convulsive embrace, and implore her in tones that would have melted the heart of a stone not to desert him, upon which, looking at her babes and remembering that it was their father who was thus pleading, she was constrained to relent and to patiently resign herself to her fate. Thus matters continued for years.

In 1863, the darling, Lottie, died of diphtheria, after an illness of only twelve hours. This sad bereavement for a while sobered Emma's companion, and, under the deepest conviction, he sincerely promised repentance. He succeeded in keeping that pledge a few months, during which time joy was in his household. Then the death angel again crossed the threshold and took the dear little boy—Allie. Strange to say, in the hour of sorrow the tempter returned, and a few short years of the most reckless debauchery terminated the life of Emma's first husband in a fit of delirium tremens, and she was left a drunkard's widow, with a mocking wraith walking beside her ever.[6] When to the crushing consciousness of the manner of the death of this partner was added the assurance of Scripture, that "no drunkard shall inherit eternal life," her sorrow seemed more than she could bear; for it is the thought of the future, more than that of the present, that moves a lofty spirit.

Such is a brief account of the inspiration of Mrs. Emma Molloy in her present great work. The author would have it distinctly understood, that he presents it, not as an *apology,* but as a *reason;* for he is not one of those who believe that if a woman has talent for public service she should put its light under a bushel to avoid the displeasure of the fossils of the age.

CHAPTER II.

SECOND MARRIAGE—BECOMES A PRINTER—THEN A LECTURER AND A MIGHTY WORKER—RESULTS OF HER WORK—SHE CAPTIVATES NEW ENGLAND—DEATH OF THE GREAT TALBOTT—OUR EMMA GOES TO GREAT BRITAIN.

In 1869,[7] Emma married her second husband, Mr. Molloy, a sober, industrious, honest, sensible man of excellent habits and broad, generous views. He was a country newspaper man, and was attracted by her sprightly contributions to the press, which often met his eye. He was publishing a weekly at the time of his marriage, and, being short of help, his little wife voluntarily went into his office, mastered the trade of a compositor with astounding readiness, and made a full hand at the case. Mr. Molloy soon made her his partner in business; and till the year 1874 she added to her domestic duties the complicated labor of type-setting, localizing, soliciting "subs" and "ads," and collecting bills; for all these things devolve upon a village editor.

At the commencement of that mysterious and wonderful movement, the Womens' Crusade, we find Mr. and Mrs. Molloy publishing a paper in Elkhart, Ind. Emma joined the very first band that was organized in that town, and enlisted for the war. It was now that she first exhibited her oratorical gifts; and in response to an invitation from South Bend, she delivered her maiden set speech[8] in Good's Opera House. To the immense audience that greated her in her native city she was introduced by the Hon. Schuyler Colfax, who presided on the occasion. As she stood before that large assembly, which was chiefly composed of old schoolmates, and, looking over the sea of upturned faces, descried many a friend of yore in whose countenance whisky had plowed the furrows of sorrow, the waves of sadness beat heavily upon the shores of her soul, and aroused to a superhuman activity all her powers of expression. She opened her mouth, and God sent words to her, such as were never before heard in that hall. She walked from the platform as one who had suddenly awaked out of a dream, and was immediately beset by hosts of enthusiastic friends, who warmly congratulated her. Among these, the most hearty, perhaps, was Mr. Colfax, who predicted for her a brilliant future and great usefulness.

Being now properly before the public, she was beset with calls from every quarter, and was soon known as one of the greatest of the many great crusaders of Indiana. Meantime she bore her full part in the trying street work of the Crusade. She was one of that noble company that was egged by Shumard and Golden, two of the dirtiest and lowest saloon-keepers in Elkhart, and was present when a fiendish rum-seller of that place, in his baffled rage, threw a cheese-box into the crowd of ladies who were praying for him, and struck sweet old Mother Henry.[9] In spirit she was a fair type of those Elkhart heroines, who stopped neither for rotten eggs nor cheese-boxes, till their victory was complete.

During the political campaign of the crusade-year (1874), Mrs. Molloy canvassed her State in behalf of the Baxter Liquor Law, after which she complied with the request of the Grand Worthy Chief of the Good Templars of Hoosierdom, to travel and speak in the interests of his order. She visited nearly every county-seat in the common-wealth, and found her temperance work pressing her so that she was compelled to give up her newspaper business, to which her excellent husband cheerfully consented.

In the Spring of 1875,[10] she went to Boston, under the auspices of Mr. J. H. Roberts, of the Lyceum Bureau of that city, and, in Tremont Temple, made her first appearance before the critical people of the Hub. The success of her performance is sufficiently indicated in the fact that she was straightway engaged by the State Alliance to make a tour of Massachusetts, and address the citizens of all its principal towns on prohibition.

This was the highest tribute to forensic power ever paid to a Western woman by any part of Yankee Land.

Having completed her task to the delight of her employers, she spent some time studying the club work which was then progressing with fine results throughout New England, and was directly over-whelmed with invitations to speak before numerous associations of reformed men. Returning home for a short visit, she accepted these calls, and again took the field in Massachusetts.

It was at this juncture that her real work began.

Hitherto, as she expresses it, she had been "hammering around the edges, but now she went to the core of the matter." What she had found Good Templary impotent to do for the inebriate, she discov-ered that the Reform Club did to perfection. She threw herself with amazing zeal and constancy into the Ribbon movement, for several months averaging eleven speeches per week, and doing an untold amount of good by personal effort. Hundreds were reclaimed in every place she visited, and the lamp of joy was relit in many a household in which it had been extinguished for years. Some of the events of the history of this period will be to her forever fragrant with beautiful memories.

One day, riding in the cars from Boston to Portsmouth, New Hampshire, she saw, in the same coach with herself, a young man in-toxicated. She went to him, and, presenting him her pledge card, said: "It may seem intrusive for a stranger to thus approach you, sir, and not exactly according to the rules of etiquette, but if I were to see you drowning, I don't think I should wait for an introduction if I could save you. And, my dear young friend, you are on the rapids which will surely drown you at last. Here is my plank, which I offer you as a means of escape."

He took the card, read it, and then very deferentially said: "Would you be seated here, madam?" She sat down by him, and learned in the course of a somewhat protracted conversation with him, that some years before he had gone from his home, in a New Hampshire village, to Boston, carrying with him the hopes of his parents, the prayers of a faithful sister, and the love of a beautiful girl to whom he was affianced. She was not a little surprised at the fullness and frankness with which he told her every thing, while in the act of which he showed her the pictures of his father's family. Upon this last exhibition of confidence she exclaimed, "O, Sir, do you know how to thank God for a mother?" looking appreciatively at the shadow of the features of the woman to whom he owed his existence. With marked tenderness he replied, "I've one of the best mothers in the world, and I'm breaking her heart."

"But where is the betrothed? I don't see her picture."

"O, I've lost her. She's gone with a *soberer* man," he answered, with a forced laugh, "and I am just simply a blot in the lives of my friends. Boston is too much for a fellow that goes there a stranger, and I was one of the fast boys that wanted to see it all, and I've fallen a prey to the leeches. My situation is gone. My money and friends took leave of me together."

"And you are going back to the old home?" asked Mrs. Molloy.

"Only for a day. I'll not bother them long," replied the young man.

In a few minutes she drew from him the fact that he was meditating suicide, and was carrying in his pocket a bottle of laudanum, intending, after he had seen his dear ones once more, to launch out for that undiscovered country where the weary travelers in the deserts of this life hope to find relief from the troubles which press them here. But before she left him he signed the pledge, and handed over to her the poison with which he had intended to take his own life.

On her return to Boston she procured him a situation through some of her friends; and to-day he is one of the most efficient Christian temperance workers in that metropolis, as the following letter, of recent date, clearly evinces:

MY DEAR FRIEND: Your letter of the 12th reached me safely, and I need not tell you how glad I was to hear from you. Do you know you seem like one of God's own good angels sent to me in just the time when I most needed a friend—a *strong* friend, who could make me feel, just as you did, my responsibility in life. Never while I live shall I cease to bless God that he sent you to me on that most desolate of days. I think the turning point in my life had come just then. It was heaven or hell, and you drifted me into the heavenly gates, and now I believe my little craft will make the port. Yes, you may tell my story, only, for the sake of the old father and mother who know nothing of the dreadful thoughts of self-destruction from which I have been snatched, please do not give my name. I am doing all I can for the Master now. I got several of my old friends down to the Friendly-Inn prayer meeting the other night, and Jennie McMasters[11] put the blue ribbon on them, and I gave them your cards. Don't forget me! Write as often as your time will permit, for your letters are a source of great strength to me, though I feel the request to be a selfish one, knowing how your time is taken.

Your own boy, JASPER.

At Athol, Massachusetts, Mrs. Molloy found in one of her night meetings a young man who was friendless and hopeless. His only living relative was an aunt, who had disowned him on account of his unbridled dissipation. When Mrs. Molloy approached him, and asked him to sign the pledge, he pulled out of his coat-pocket a flask of liquor, and, with an air of desperate bravado, asked her how he could take the obligation with that in his hand. Very kindly she said to him, "You would better go with me to the door and throw it away, and begin from to-night to lead a new life." And, as she proceeded further to gently remonstrate with him, and, by way of appeal, mentioned his mother, the fountain of tenderness was unsealed, his lip quivered, the tears came dropping down over his face, and he said:

"O, Mrs. Molloy, I know better than to live as I am living. I promised my dear old mother on her death bed to be a better boy, and this is the way I have kept my word. I will not sign your pledge to-night. I am not in a fit condition to do it. But, with your permission, I will come and see you to-morrow, and we will talk the matter over."

Early the next morning he came to the house where she was stopping, in great distress of mind, imploring her to pray for him. Of course, she wrestled with God in his behalf. For three days he was in the valley and shadow of humiliation, and, at last, on his knees before God, voluntarily renounced liquor, tobacco, and profanity. He then put on the tri-colored badge.

While Mrs. Molloy was satisfied that this young man was converted, she feared that the withdrawal of the stimulus of both alcohol and tobacco might produce serious results, for he had long been an excessive drinker and an extravagant chewer. So she sent him to her friend, Dr. Day, of the Boston Washingtonian Home, who, she knew, would give him proper medical attention; for she is one of those who understand that there is such a thing as an alcoholic disease, which can not be cured by spiritual treatment alone. From this young man, who is now doing much good in turning others away from their sins, she subsequently received the letter now presented:

BOSTON WASHINGTONIAN HOME.

MY MORE THAN MOTHER. I arrived here safely, though sick, and weak, but the moment I looked in the face of Dr. Day, I felt he could understand me. I told him you were afraid he would advise me to begin using tobacco again, but he just laid his hand on my head in such a fatherly way, that I felt as though he would help me through, even before he said it; and now I am happy to tell you that he says that a few days will bring me out all right. My nervous system is fearfully shattered, but he is giving me tonics to build me up. I am using the "Blanchard's Food and Nerve Cure" you gave me, and feel better already. I am only worried about one thing, and that is the money you have paid out for me; but I hope soon to get to work and repay it to you. I am sure you will find that your confidence in me was not in vain; I shall make the battle, or die trying. Do take good care of your health, my dear friend. It frightens me to see how hard you are working. If you should die, I should have no one in all the world who understands me, for, since my mother died, until you found me, I have been utterly

alone in the world. I am praying for you in my feeble way. Do not forget me in your petitions. I am sure "He is able to carry me through."
Your own boy, ALFRED.

I have here given but two out of hundreds of cases of unfortunate persons whom this grand little woman has rescued from the very brink of eternal destruction, often wading through the slime and filth of the gutter to accomplish her task. Who shall say that a lady dishonors her sex in following Jesus, as Lydia and Phoebe[12] did, into the dark, thorny, marshy by-ways and hedges in search of the poor lost sheep of the Great Shepherd? People who object to the performance of such missions are not only as blind as bats to the plainest lessons of the New Testament, but are utterly ignorant of the meaning of the word, lady, which in its old Saxon form, "*lafdean,*" signified loaf-distributer, having been originally applied to those noble wives and daughters of the feudal age, who, in a period of famine left their luxuriant manor-houses, and carried bread to the multitudes of starving peasants who pressed upon the English Barons with the cry—"lo-ard! lo-ard!" which latter meant "loaf-afford! loaf-afford!" and which in process of time was contracted into our common term, "lord," and is most appropriately used to designate Him through whom the bread of life comes down from Heaven. The two nouns, lord and lady, are now more abused than almost any others in the language. It is the noblest thing in the world to be a lady indeed.

Mrs. Molloy remained in Massachusetts, now and then making short visits to other New England States, till July, 1876, when the very pleasant and highly commendatory affair, a notice of which I clip from the Boston *Globe*, occurred:

FAREWELL RECEPTION TO MRS. EMMA MOLLOY.

Mrs. Emma Molloy, who has lectured upon temperance in Massachusetts with great success for the past two months, leaves for her home in Indiana to-day. Yesterday afternoon a farewell reception was given her in Wesleyan Hall by her friends. The company included many of the leading workers in the temperance cause, and a social hour was spent very pleasantly. Brief addresses were made by several of those present, all testifying to their high estimation of Mrs. Molloy's services and their regret that she was to leave the State, and giving her the assurance of a hearty and cordial welcome when she returns. Letters speaking of her services in the warmest terms were read from Mrs. Mary A. Livermore, Wendell Phillips, the Hon. John I. Baker, H. D. Cushing, Esq.,[13] and others. Mrs. Molloy expects to return here in September and to participate in the political campaign. During the past two months about two thousands persons, including many of the hardest drinkers, have signed the pledge at her meetings.

During this reception, the Hon. Henry Faxon,[14] on behalf of certain appreciative citizens of the Hub, presented Mrs. Molloy with $100.

She now returned home, to Indiana, to suffer one of the most painful losses of her life. In a letter to the author, speaking of that melancholy event, she says:

The Rev. J. J. Talbott, the temperance Demosthenes of the Northwest, and long the honored Worthy Chief of the Good Templars of Indiana, who had been like a brother to me in my work, smoothing many a rugged place for me, and cheering me often when I was discouraged, aiding me by his wider and riper experience, had fallen again. It was a terrible blow. I had never thought it possible that he could drink again, and nothing in all my work had so unnerved me as this. He came to my house and for weeks my husband and myself watched over him as we would have watched with a sick child. During this illness we talked much about the work and our future prospects, and upon his bed, Oh! how solemnly and earnestly he consecrated himself to God, praying to be restored to health once more that he might wipe the stain of defeat from his record. But God saw fit to take him away from all this trial and temptation. As the moment of dissolution drew near he looked up tenderly and said, "It is not right to weep for me! Isn't it better to be lifted out of all trouble and find peace, peace? I leave in your hands my unfinished work. Be faithful to the end, and we shall meet over there. The June roses will not blossom many times between us, and when you are lonely and weary remember that Jerry will be watching and waiting at the beautiful gate for you." And so, just as the morning was spread upon the mountains; as day opened her golden gates with rosy fingers, the beautiful spirit of "our Jerry" burst its prison of clay and, unfettered, entered its spirit home. We took him to New Albany and laid him beside his mother; and as the clods of the valley fell upon his dear form, we felt that they were covering one who, though bound to us by no ties of blood, was spiritually our kindred. I am more than glad to add this little tribute to the memory of one who so faithfully labored for others and strove to retrieve all the wrong he had committed by faithful service in the cause of the Master. His weary feet, that sometimes wandered and were pierced by the thorns of his mistakes, are at last at rest. Death smoothed from his face all the furrows of care, and left a look of unutterable peace upon it; and by this token we believe that God's mercy, which is wide and boundless as the far reaching universe, has rolled the mists from his soul and given him eternal bliss.

The author well remembers hearing Mr. Talbott, in the Summer of 1856, at Indianapolis, deliver a speech which that distinguished war horse, Prof. Ryland T. Brown,[15] pronounced the most splendid effort he had ever heard in his life. He was truly a man of superior gifts, and his blood, to-day, cries from the ground against the infernal traffic that murdered him.

In the Fall of 1876, Mrs. Molloy went back to Massachusetts, and thoroughly canvassed the State in support of the State ticket put in nomination that year by the Prohibition party. The ability with which she handled the issues of the campaign astonished even her most enthusiastic admirers, and completely dumfounded her opponents. Much of the time she was accompanied by the Rev. George Vibbert,[16] whose motto, *"Peace if possible, justice at any rate,"* she still carries in her autograph album and often exhibits with pride. She wound up her political canvass of the Bay State at East Boston, at a mass-meeting in which she followed the renowned Wendell Phillips, in one of the most thrilling and powerful appeals ever heard in America. The following notice from the Boston *Herald* will give the reader some idea of the effect of this speech:

THE PROHIBITIONISTS OF EAST BOSTON

held their final rally Saturday evening. Sumner Hall was crowded to its utmost capacity, upwards of one thousand eight hundred people being present. Cornelius Lovell, Esq., Prohibitory candidate for Senator from the First Suffolk District, presided, and introduced as the first speaker, Wendell Phillips. Mr. Phillips delivered substantially the speech made by him, on Thursday evening, at the Highlands, already reported, and at its close he was warmly applauded. Mrs. Emma Molloy, of Indiana, was the last speaker, and she made a most stirring and eloquent appeal to the voters present to support on Tuesday the Prohibitory State ticket, and thus inaugurate a policy that shall stop the terrible tide of demoralization now fostered by the dram-shop. While Mr. Phillips made the solid argument for prohibition, Mrs. Molloy made the direct appeal to the voters, and wrought her audience to the highest pitch of enthusiasm. The meeting is accounted a grand success by the Prohibition leaders in East Boston, and they feel confident it will tend to greatly swell the Baker and Eddy[17] vote.

From the Autumn of 1876 till the present hour Mrs. Molloy has labored constantly throughout the Union as a Ribbon worker, and has rescued many thousands of souls from the fatal meshes of intemperance. No missionary was ever actuated by purer, loftier motives. She cares not one poor straw for the color of the ribbon with which the devil is shot. Nor does she care who has the honor of the shooting. All she wants is to see him routed.

During the Summer of the present year (1878) she received a call from Great Britain, which she promptly accepted. In September she set sail for that part of the world; and our English cousins will be waked up by the little Hoosier woman as they were never before waked up on the subject of temperance.

She is, in a peculiar sense, America's pride, as she will be England's delight. Her eloquence gushes spontaneously from the fountain of a bitter experience, and its deep fervor, exquisite pathos, and irresistible power, can not be excelled in any quarter of the globe. She has already done vastly more for mankind than mankind can ever do for her; but when the last trump shall sound, and the dead, small and great, shall stand before the Infinite One, the Friend of Martha and Mary—the Elder Brother of all true-hearted workers—shall bring forth a white robe, and a crown, and handing them to her and pointing to a host of blood-washed spirits who were saved through her instrumentality, shall say, "Reign in peace and joy forever, thou triumphant queen of many grateful hearts."

NOTES

Preface and Acknowledgements

1. "Emma Barrett Molloy, South Bend's Early-Day Liberationist," *South Bend Tribune,* Aug. 31, 1975. A monograph, *Women in Elkhart A Century Ago (*1978) also drew upon the *Observer.*

Chapter 1

1. There were, however, other female Hoosier newspaper writers. The *South Bend National Union* mentions Minnie Rizer of Lafayette (Nov. 12, 1870), Laura Ream of Indianapolis (Sept. 30, 1870), and an unnamed editor of the *Covington Friend* (Mar. 25, 1871). Elizabeth Boynton (Harbert), later editor of "Woman's Kingdom" for the *Chicago Inter-Ocean,* was a correspondent for the *Indianapolis Journal* (the *Agitator,* Sept. 18, 1869, p. 1). The *South Bend National Union* has been preserved by the Northern Indiana Historical Society, South Bend; the *Elkhart Observer* by the Elkhart County Historical Society, Bristol. The *Observer* also has been microfilmed by the Indiana Newspaper Project.

Chapter 2

1. Accounts of Emma's early life and family may be found in "The Life of Mrs. Emma Molloy" in James M. Hiatt, *The Ribbon Workers* (Chicago, 1878), p. 284-85; obituary of Emma Molloy Barrett, *South Bend Times,* May 15, 1907; obituary of William L. Barrett, *ibid.,* Mar. 29, 1899; sketch of William L. Barrett, Anderson and Cooley, *South Bend and the Men Who Have Made It* (South Bend, 1901), p. 238-39; "Record of the Barrett Family," typescript, 1879, owned by J. Barrett Guthrie; "A Family Camp-Meeting," *Livingston Republican,* Geneseo, New York, July 3, 1879. The family's roots are in New England.
2. Evidence of her parents' activities in First Methodist Episcopal Church, South Bend Station, Record 1838-1843, and South Bend Union Sabbath School, Record 1835-1869, p. 75 (at the Northern Indiana Historical Society, South Bend). More on her mother in Hiatt, *Ribbon Workers,* p. 284-85; *Cherokee Advocate,* Tahlequah, Oklahoma, Dec. 14, 1883. Hiatt quotes from a letter of Harriett Newton Barrett apparently in Emma's possession at that time.
3. According to "Record of the Barrett Family" (see note 1), Emma had two siblings, Clement Barrett (Apr. 4, 1837-Sept. 2, 1838) and Eliza H. Barrett (May 13-June 4, 1841), and her mother died May 28, 1841. Emma's attendance at her mother's funeral: "On the Road," *Elkhart Observer,* July 1, 1874. According to Hiatt, *Ribbon Workers,* p. 285, Emma boarded out eleven years, but this account is prone to exaggeration. Her father's work in Chicago is mentioned in *South Bend and the Men Who Have Made It,* p. 239; *Chicago City Directory...1849-*

50, p. 73; *Danenhower's Chicago City Directory for 1851*, p. 21; *Good Templars' Watchword* (UK.), Oct. 9, 1878, p. 657.

4. Obituary of George Bryson, *South Bend National Union*, Dec. 21, 1867. The Brysons had property in both St. Joseph and Elkhart Counties. Emma is listed with Burroughs in South Bend in Portage Township School Enumerations, 1846-48 (Northern Indiana Historical Society). George Bryson is mentioned in records of the Elkhart Circuit, Goshen District, Northern Indiana Conference (at St. Paul's United Methodist Church, Elkhart). Their household and her tasks are described by Emma in "The Old Home," *North Iowa Times*, McGregor, Sept. 23, 1863; "An Autumn Dream," *Wisconsin Democrat*, Madison, Nov. 18, 1865; "Thanksgiving," *South Bend National Union*, Nov. 30, 1867; "March," *ibid.*, Mar. 7, 1868. It is not known where else she may have boarded. Her grandmother, Susannah Newton Hackney, may be one possibility.

5. Emma's South Bend district school attendance is mentioned in a diary of Asa Cyrus Call, Mss. 301, p. 29 (California Historical Society); Portage Township School Enumerations, 1846-48 (Northern Indiana Historical Society). Items on Sophia Bookstaver, *South Bend National Union*, Apr. 22, 1871; Flora Shively Beitner, "Some Early Schools of South Bend, Indiana," *Old Courthouse News*, Winter/Spring, 1984.

6. Her attendance is verified in First Methodist Episcopal Church, Sunday School Auxiliary Record, Jan. 5, 1852 (Northern Indiana Historical Society); Roll Books, 1835-46 and 1851-64 and Female Bible Class Record, 1852-58 (First United Methodist Church, South Bend). Attitudes noted in *Sunday School Advocate*, 1846-50 (Northwestern University Library). Mary F. Burroughs death: City Cemetery Records, South Bend, Part I, p. 4.

7. Items on William Barrett's property and family in St. Joseph County (Indiana) Recorder, Deed Record, Book R, p. 85, Oct. 15, 1852; Portage Township Assessor's Book, 1856 (Northern Indiana Historical Society); burial records, South Bend City Cemetery; U S. Census Population Schedules, St. Joseph County, Indiana, 1870, p. 448. For names/dates of their children see Emma's Family pages. William Barrett described by C. N. Fassett ("Recollections of William L. Barrett," Barrett genealogy file, Northern Indiana Historical Society). His store, Fassett noted, was on the site of the later Wyman's.

8. *Good Templars' Watchword* (UK.), Oct. 9, 1878, p. 657. Some of Emma's early stories strongly hint at a difficult relationship with her stepmother. There is no documentation in Beitner's article (Note 5) for a statement that Mrs. Barrett ran a school for girls on Michigan Street.

9. Impact of *Uncle Tom's Cabin:* Charles H. Bartlett, "A Narrative of South Bend, 1844-65," *Old Courthouse News*, Winter 1968. With her lively books and columns, Sara Payson Willis Parton ("Fanny Fern") (1811-72) inspired many girls to consider careers. *Ruth Hall* described by Emma Molloy, *Elkhart Observer*, Oct. 23, 1872. Influence of "domestic novel": Helen W. Papashvily, *All the Happy Endings...* (New York, 1956). Feminist reformers apparently did not inspire Emma at this age.

10. *St. Joseph County Forum*, South Bend, Apr. 1, 1854; *St. Joseph Valley Register*, South Bend, Apr. 12, 1855; obituary of Frances E. Grether, *South Bend National Union*, May 23, 1868; *St. Joseph County Forum*, Jan. 10, 1857.

11. Items on teaching: *South Bend National Union*, Feb. 20, 1869; *St. Joseph County Forum*, June 21, 1856; *North Iowa Times*, Feb. 10, 1858; *Good Templars' Watchword*, Oct. 9, 1878, p. 657. Location of the country school, if traced from Census records on a former pupil, Francis M. Jackson (mentioned in *National Union*, 1869 item cited above), was Warren Township west of South Bend.

12. Quote from "Home," *St. Joseph Valley Register*, Feb. 7, 1856. Other "Histories": *ibid.*, Jan. 17, Feb. 28, Mar. 20, 1856. Emma's authorship confirmed by series title (same as 1859 story), subject matter, dramatic presentation, opinions, names. Women's power in secrecy: Carolyn Heilbrun, *Writing a Woman's Life* (New York, 1988), p. 110-117. Though Emma was said to have published writings at twelve or thirteen, the first items found that looked possibly to be hers were in 1854 and 1855.

13. Information on this period is very inadequate. Emma's teaching in the South at seventeen is described in *Elgin* (Illinois) *News*, Nov. 21, 1883. Her early story describes in detail student life in a southern girls' college ("Answering an Advertisement," *North Iowa Times*, McGregor, Iowa, Oct. 12, 1859). Barretts in Montgomery: Hiatt, *Ribbon Workers*, p. 288; Barrett family history, Milo B. Howard papers, Alabama Department of Archives and History; Montgomery city directories. Emma and Morris Barrett were engaged in their youth: *Pacific Christian Advocate*, Jan. 10, 1889, p. 8. Emma's first essay in *North Iowa Times:* "Memory," Nov. 23, 1857.

14. "Good-bye," *ibid.*, Feb. 10, 1858.

Chapter 3

1. Two examples on friends: "To M.E.I.," *Wisconsin Capitol*, May 10, 1865; "An Autumn Dream," *Wisconsin Democrat*, Nov. 18, 1865. They profile a close girl friend and "Hal," an older boy who died young. Distrust of men: "Answer to Migap," *St. Joseph County Forum*, Sept. 19, 1857; "To-Morrow," *North Iowa Times*, Dec. 30, 1857; "Heart Histories." How she met Pradt is unknown; perhaps through his sister Charlotte J. Pradt, who taught in the South and published stories in the *North Iowa Times;* or even by correspondence ("Answering an Advertisement"). Marriage: St. Joseph County Marriage Record, Book 4, p. 146 (Apr. 8, 1858).

2. Pradt's family is documented in U S. Census, Windham County, Vermont, 1850, p. 73; *History of Dane County, Wisconsin* (Chicago, 1880), p. 1022-23; *Sheboygan* (Illinois) *Journal*, Feb. 18, 1858. Emma's distress is described in Hiatt, *Ribbon Workers*, p. 186-90, and Dane County Clerk's Records, Emma Pradt vs. Louis Pradt, 1867.

3. Approximate times of their moves indicated by "Grammar," *Mishawaka* (Indiana) *Enterprise*, Jan. 22, 1859; "A Heart History," *ibid.*, Oct. 15, 1859; Hiatt, *Ribbon Workers*, p. 288-89; U S. Census, Montgomery County, Alabama, 1860, p. 193; *History of Dane County, Wisconsin*, p. 1023. Fired for his drinking: Hiatt, *Ribbon Workers*, p. 288. Children's birth months indicated in *Wisconsin State Journal*, Madison, Oct. 24, 1863, Aug. 18, 1864, and *Wisconsin Patriot*, Madison, Dec. 31, 1863.

4. Louis Pradt is listed as a member in Madison Typographical Union, Charter and By-laws (State Historical Society of Wisconsin). Emma's efforts detailed in Hiatt, *Ribbon Workers*, p. 288; *Woman's Journal*, Nov. 28, 1874, p. 380; article on Abby Sage McFarland Richardson in *Elkhart Observer*, Dec. 11, 1872. Remarks on "fifteen years" of servant problems in account of Anna Dickinson lecture, *ibid.*, Apr. 2, 1873.

5. "Soul-Clouds and Soul-Light," *Wisconsin Patriot*, Feb. 25, 1862.

6. "My Angel Guest," *ibid.*, May 10, 1862. Outrage against husbands expressed in a story on the death of "Ella Lee," *ibid.*, May 2, 1863. One of many pieces on deaths of children: "Only a Lock of Hair," *ibid.*, Feb. 14, 1863.

7. Emile Barton Cary, a longtime friend, is described as related by marriage to the writers Alice and Phoebe Cary, in *South Bend National Union*, Oct. 7, 1871. Emma and Emile were still friends in 1886: *Fort Wayne News*, May 10, 1886. Her obituary: *LaCygne*, (Kansas) *Weekly*

Journal, Apr. 12, 1912. (Lucius Cary founded a newspaper in LaCygne.) Church member-ship: Parish Register, 1847-1900, Grace Episcopal Church, Sheboygan; Edith T. Emery, *Records of the First Methodist Episcopal Church of Madison, Wisconsin, 1853-1870* (Madison, 1929), p. 141-42. In Madison, Emma Pradt accompanied Helene Hastreiter, later a well-known singer: *South Bend National Union,* Oct. 3, 1868.

8. "Cast Thy Burden on the Lord," *Wisconsin Daily Patriot,* Feb. 17, 1864. "This cruel war" refers to a universally known Civil War era song, "Weeping, Sad and Lonely." Deaths: *Wisconsin State Journal,* Oct. 24, 1863, Aug. 18, 1864; *Mishawaka Enterprise,* Aug. 20, 1864; "New Year's Eve," *Wisconsin Patriot,* Dec. 31, 1863; *South Bend Tribune,* July 23, 1886. Oddly, she published a poem on a child's death using the name Allie a year before her Allie's death: "Allie," *Wisconsin Daily Patriot,* Aug. 21, 1863.

9. "The Polly Wiggins Letters," *Wisconsin Capitol,* Aug. 8, 1865.

10. "The Polly Wiggins Letters," *Wisconsin Capitol,* Feb. 14, 1866; others appeared in *ibid.* on Aug. 4, 12, 18, 28, Sept. 5, 22, Oct. 9, Nov. 3, 1865; Feb. 5, Mar. 6, 14, Apr. 4, 1866; and in the *Wisconsin Union,* Madison, May 9, 1866. Bill described in *Wisconsin Capitol,* Mar. 7, 15, 1866. Emma Pradt is identified as "Polly Wiggins" in *St. Joseph Valley Register,* June 28, 1866.

11. *Wisconsin Capitol,* Mar. 6, 13, 15, 24, 1866

Chapter 4

1. Teaching: Phebe Hanaford, *Women of the Century* (Boston, 1877), p. 674; *South Bend National Union,* June 8, 1867. Divorce: Dane County, Wisconsin Clerk's Records, Emma Pradt vs. Louis Pradt, 1867. Later, in lecturing, she would give the strong impression she had been widowed. *The Ribbon Workers* (p. 290) refers to Louis' death coming shortly after the children's deaths (1863-64). Though possibly he died very shortly after the divorce no data could be found. Local people knew of her divorce: *Goshen Democrat,* Apr. 8, 1874. She appeared on an early attendance list, but was not a communicant at St. James Episcopal Church, South Bend: Parish Register 1 (Cathedral of St. James, South Bend).

2. Concert: *St. Joseph Valley Register,* May 16, 1867. Her writings included "Mrs. Stubbs Letters" (written in "Polly Wiggins" style), *ibid.,* May 30, June 20, July 11, Aug. 1, 1867; oth-ers under her own name; under pseudonym "Mabel Clare": *ibid.,* May 25, Oct. 5, 1867.

3. Description of Edward Molloy: obituaries in *Indiana Magazine of History,* v. X (June, 1914), p. 88, and *LaPorte Herald,* Mar. 18, 1914. His early temperance vows are described in *Good Templars' Watchword,* Oct. 9, 1878, p. 657. The quote is from Hiatt, *Ribbon Workers,* p. 291.

4. St. Joseph County Marriage Record, Book 5, p. 548, Nov. 28, 1867. The *Register* accused them of taking a "honeymoon" before marriage: Dec. 19, 1867.

5. Her thoughts on women as good "country journalists" are in her address to the sec-ond Woman's Congress (*Woman's Journal,* Nov. 28, 1874, p. 380); in Hanaford, *Women of the Century,* p. 674-75.

6. "The Editress Wishes to Hire a Girl," *South Bend National Union,* July 25, 1868. See also "Answers to Our Ad," *ibid.,* Aug. 8, 1868; "Moving," *ibid.,* Dec. 5, 1868. Hired girl listed with Molloys in US. Census, St. Joseph County, Indiana, 1870, p. 104.

7. *Holland's Directory, 1867-68* places the *Union* office on the north side of Washing-ton St. just east of the corner of Main. Pictures: "Pictures," *South Bend National Union,* Jan. 18, 1868.

8. "Our Collecting Tour," *ibid.,* Nov. 28, 1868; *ibid.,* Jan. 9, 1869; *Woman's Journal,* Nov.

28, 1874, p. 380; Hanaford, *Women of the Century*, p. 674.

9. Success of *South Bend National Union*: *St. Joseph Valley Register*, Dec. 28, 1871. Editors' meetings: *South Bend National Union*, Jan. 9, Oct. 23, 1869; Apr. 23, 1870; Apr. 22, 1871.

10. Items on Normal Musical Institute in *ibid.*, Oct. 30, 1869, Apr. 9, 1870, July 23, 1870, Aug. 13, 20, 1870; on Clark, *ibid.*, May 8, July 3, 1869; *Elkhart Observer*, Oct. 14, 1874; *Port Townsend Daily Leader*, July 5, 1891. For decades, Clark presented popular solo programs, appearing at many temperance meetings, including some organized by Emma. He also was a writer.

11. Her book manuscript still existed in 1875, according to Higgins, Belden & Co., *An Illustrated Historical Atlas of St. Joseph County, Indiana* (Chicago, 1875), p. 10. Among many notices of it, *South Bend National Union*, Mar. 6, 1869, Apr. 15, 1871; *Elkhart Observer*, Apr. 9, 1873. What became of it is unknown.

12. New York: *South Bend National Union*, June 27, July 25, Aug. 8, 1868; poem "Greetings to the White Boys in Blue," *ibid.*, Aug. 8, 1868. Reunions: *First Annual Reunion...of the 87th Indiana Volunteer Infantry* (South Bend, 1870), p. 24-28; *South Bend National Union*, Oct. 2, 1869; *Rochester* (Indiana) *Union Spy*, Sept. 23, 1870; *South Bend National Union*, Sept. 23, 1871.

13. Reference to *Sorosis*: *South Bend National Union*, Jan. 16, 1869; visit to Stanton/ Anthony: *ibid.*, Aug. 8, 1868.

14. Some editorials: "The Insincerity of Social Life," *ibid.*, Dec. 21, 1867; pro-suffrage comments, *ibid.*, Nov. 13, 27, 1869, Feb. 6, Apr. 2, May 28, Aug. 6, 1870; Feb. 18, Mar. 4, Apr. 8, 1871. Employment of women: *ibid.*, Mar. 4, 1871; *Woman's Journal*, Jan. 14, 1871, p. 9.

15. Quote from "Free Love," *South Bend National Union*, May 28, 1870. The title must have tempted the gossips, especially since in that issue she expressed best wishes to Victoria Woodhull, a famed "free love" advocate, on her new editorial venture. Second editorial on the case, *ibid.*, June 25, 1870. Emma wrote that she knew Richardson when both were copyists in the same Madison office (*ibid.*, May 28, 1870). She also wrote that she had been acquainted with Clara Barton (*ibid.*, Mar. 14, 1868). Editorials against abusive men: *ibid.*, Sept. 25, 1869, June 4, 1870.

16. "Aunt Nabby" letter, *ibid.*, June 17, 1871; others on July 15, Aug. 5, 1871.

17. Editorials on temperance: *ibid.*, Feb. 18, Mar. 11, 1871.

18. *The Revolution*, Jan. 28, 1869, p. 51; other "Pat Molloy" pieces, Apr. 15, p. 236; Dec. 9, p. 355-56. "Mrs. Petroleum V. Nasby" articles, probably by Emma, on Aug. 26, p. 114; Sept. 9, p. 145-46; Sept. 30, p. 193.

19. Her attendance noted by Elizabeth Cady Stanton and Susan B. Anthony in *A History of Woman Suffrage* (Rochester, 1886) v. III, p. 570; *Chicago Times*, Sept. 11, 1869; the *Agitator*, Sept. 18, 1869, p. 4. At this convention she witnessed the conflict between the two wings of the woman suffrage movement. Typically independent, over the years she would participate in both.

20. Her lectures described in *LaPorte* (Indiana) *Argus*, Jan. 20, 1870; *Ligonier* (Indiana) *National Banner*, Feb. 9, 16, 1870; *Elkhart Review*, Feb. 3, 1870; *St. Joseph Valley Register*, Feb. 3, 1870; *South Bend National Union*, Feb. 19, 1870; *Rochester* (Indiana) *Union Spy*, Mar. 10, 1871; *South Bend National Union*, Mar. 11, 18, 1871. Mary Livermore had spoken on a theme very similar to Emma's 1870 talk during the Woman Suffrage Association of Indiana's annual meeting (*Indianapolis Journal*, June 9, 1869), which Emma did not attend but knew about. Emma's acquaintance with Livermore: see Chapter 5, Note 14.

21. *Harper's Bazaar,* Mar. 26, 1870, p. 195. Also noted in *Woman's Journal,* Mar. 19, 1870, p. 85. Emma herself later often sent out notices; it is not known if she did in this case.

22. *South Bend National Union,* June 18, 1870.

23. *Ibid.,* Aug. 13, 1870.

24. *South Bend National Union,* Aug. 27, Nov. 12, 19, 26, Dec. 3, 10, 24, 1870.

Chapter 5

1. "Beyond the Mississippi," *South Bend National Union,* July 15, 1871. Also, Emile Cary and her husband had moved to Kansas.

2. "A Day in Indianapolis," *ibid.,* June 3, 1871. The northern Indiana group apparently was not connected with the state association. The Molloys also were members of the latter in 1871: *Articles of Association and Complete Record...of the Editors and Publishers Association of Indiana* (Indianapolis, 1871), p. 29 (Indiana Historical Society Library). Western excursion described in *South Bend National Union,* July 15, 1871; praise of male colleagues: *Woman's Journal,* Nov. 28, 1874, p. 380.

3. "Gossiping," *South Bend National Union,* Nov. 12, 1870; others, "Miss Sharpnose," *ibid.,* May 9, 1868; "Free Love," *ibid.,* May 28, 1870; "Aunt Mary's Story," *ibid.,* Jan. 28, 1871; "Aunt Nabby," *ibid.,* June 17, 1871.

4. Account of fire: "Chicago," *ibid.,* Oct. 21, 1871. Items concerning leaving South Bend and going to Cortland: *ibid.,* Dec. 9, 1871; *St. Joseph Valley Register,* Dec. 28, 1871, Jan. 11, 1872. The Molloys' reasons for changing their politics are not known, nor are their particular connnections in Cortland. The *Cortland Journal* has not been preserved.

5. *Cortland* (New York) *Standard,* May 3, 1883, May 7, 1872; *South Bend Tribune,* May 18, 1872. Emma's illness: *South Bend Tribune,* June 22, 1872; *Elkhart Observer,* Aug. 21, 1872. Illness is given as the reason for giving up the paper in Phebe Hanaford, *Women of the Century,* p. 675.

6. Items on start of *Elkhart Observer, ibid.,* Aug. 21, 1872; *Elkhart Review,* July 18, Aug. 1, 1872.

7. Dr. Miles founded his company, now part of Bayer, in 1884. Their river trip: *Elkhart Observer,* Sept. 24, Oct. 1, 8, 1873. It was especially daring because it was the malarial season.

8. Aid society: *ibid.,* Nov. 27, Dec. 4, 1872, Jan. 15, 1873. Eastern Star: *ibid.,* Feb. 11, 1874. Opera house opening: *ibid.,* Jan. 1, 1873. Performance: *ibid.,* Jan. 1, 1873. History: see Chapter 4, Note 11.

Etta: *ibid.,* Nov. 5, 1872; *Springfield Express* (Missouri), June 17, 1887; U S. Census, LaPorte County, Indiana, 1880, p. 192, where Etta is listed as a domestic/nurse. A letter written by Etta, owned by her great-granddaughter, Jean Hass of Creswell, Oregon, describes the name change and states she was adopted. All her adult life, Emma tended to offer a home to others. Surely she felt a sense of mission in taking in her adopted and foster daughters, as she herself had been taken in. But they were expected to do housework. "Mary," a domestic worker, was mentioned frequently in Emma's household column. In 1873, their household included Frank, Etta, "Grace" and "Auntie," according to "Housekeeper's Diary," *Elkhart Observer,* Nov. 5, 1873.

9. Robert K. Brush (1823-1910) was one of Lincoln's very late appointees, serving as Elkhart's postmaster from 1865 to 1875. (From obituary owned by his descendant, the Rev. George M. Minnix of Elkhart.) Locations of *Observer: ibid.,* Aug. 21, 1872, Aug. 6, 1873. Quote from *Goshen Democrat,* Aug. 5, 1873.

10. "To Kansas and Return," *Elkhart Observer,* Nov. 27, 1872; *LaCygne Weekly Journal,*

Nov. 16, 1872.

11. "The Hearthstone," *Elkhart Observer,* Dec. 24, 1873. These columns were based in part on her own household diaries.

12. "Can Women Obtain Justice?", *ibid.,* Nov. 27, 1872; "About Justice to Women," Dec. 11, 1872; "What Women Are Doing in Elkhart," *ibid.,* May 28, 1873. Dickinson: *ibid.,* Apr. 2, 1872; Livermore: *ibid.,* Feb. 18, 25, Mar. 4, 1874; Richardson: *ibid.,* Dec. 31, 1873, Jan. 7, 1874; Stanton: *ibid.,* Nov. 17, 1872, Dec. 10, 1873. Possibly Emma helped arrange some of the lectures.

13. "About Women," *Elkhart Observer,* Apr. 30, 1873.

14. *Ibid.,* Feb. 18, 1874. Though letters between the two have not been found, it seems possible that Mary Ashton Rice Livermore (1820-1905) aided Emma Molloy in her career. They may have met at the Western Woman Suffrage Convention in 1869. During Livermore's editorship of the *Woman's Journal,* Emma's work as editor was noted (see Chapter 4, Note 21), and a *National Union* article on a female typesetter was reprinted (Jan. 14, 1871, p. 9). They may have became better acquainted during Livermore's lectures in South Bend and Goshen in 1874. From then on there are several possible connections. Livermore's testimonials on Emma's behalf in 1878 (Chapter 7) evidence acquaintance and mutual esteem.

15. Her typesetters are described in "What Women Are Doing in Elkhart," *Elkhart Observer,* May 28, 1873. Printers' stories of her bossiness recounted in *Elkhart Sentinel,* Mar. 6, 1886.

16. *Woman's Journal,* Nov. 28, 1874, p. 380.

17. References to her practice of spiritualism while in Elkhart in *Goshen Democrat,* June 17, 1874; *Elkhart Sentinel,* Mar. 6, 1886; *Elkhart Review,* Apr. 7, 1886. Though spiritualism was "in vogue," it seems to have been more than a matter of curiosity for her. The later accounts, written when the vogue had passed, are by opponents and may be magnified in their details. One describes her going into a medium-like trance to "channel" the spirit of a black man. Franklin Miles, their friend, also was much interested in spiritualism ("The Davenport Brothers," *Elkhart Observer,* Dec. 18, 1872).

Her attack is described in *Elkhart Review,* May 15, 1873 and *Elkhart Democratic Union,* May 16, 1873. The former account reads: "Mrs. Molloy was suddenly seized with terrible convulsions, while about her usual occupations, yesterday afternoon. She passed rapidly from one spasm into another, and notwithstanding the fact that three men were holding her, she succeeded in severely bruising and scratching herself..." In sources describing her later travels, at least three other accounts of swooning or convulsive attacks were found, along with many mentions of unspecified illness. In one of these attacks, Emma fell to the floor while preaching. (*Weekly Bedrock Democrat,* Baker City, Oregon, Feb. 4, 1889).

Chapter 6

1. *Battle Creek Journal,* May 6, 1874. For a history of the woman's temperance movement, see Ruth Bordin, *Woman and Temperance* (Philadelphia, 1981).

2. *Elkhart Observer,* Mar. 19, 26, 1873; *ibid,* Dec. 3, 1873.

3. *Ibid.,* Mar. 4, 1874. Emma much admired "Mother" Stewart, one of the early Crusade leaders.

4. Emma's report and editorial on the start of the Elkhart crusade: *ibid.,* Mar. 25, 1874. Her role in devising strategy: *Bridgewater Mercury* (UK.), Nov. 27, 1878. Local accounts of the Crusade appear in newspapers throughout northern Indiana and in Chapman, *History of*

St. Joseph County, Indiana (Chicago, 1880), p. 582-85. Elkhart Crusade: Pickrell, *Women in Elkhart a Century Ago* and Molloy article, *South Bend Tribune,* Aug. 31, 1975.

5. Many items in the *Elkhart Observer* follow her Crusade work. Rally with Colfax: *St. Joseph Valley Register,* Mar. 19, 1874. Indiana papers: *LaPorte Argus,* Apr. 2, 1874; *Plymouth Republican,* Apr. 2, 9, 1874; *Goshen Democrat,* Apr. 8, 15, 1874; *Valparaiso Vidette,* Apr. 23, 30, 1874; *Niles (Michigan) Republican,* Apr. 23, 1874; *Harvard (Illinois) Independent,* May 6, 27, 1874; *Albion College Annalist,* May 14, 1874.

6. Frances E. Willard, Letter to Annie Wittenmeyer, May 24, 1876, Temperance and Prohibition Papers, WCTU Series, Sec. II, Roll 11, p. 518-19—the one letter pertaining to Emma Molloy that could be found. The two do not appear to have become friends. There may be a touch of envy in Willard's letter: it ends, "...In Indianapolis she swept things before her—I felt like a rush light!" They were involved in many of the same meetings and had contact through the WCTU and through temperance journals.

7. *Niles Republican,* Apr. 23, 1874. A few of many descriptions of her oratory: *Summit County* (Ohio) *Beacon,* July 8, 1874; *Indianapolis Journal,* Mar. 1, 1875; *South Bend Tribune,* June 3, 1876. She credited her oratorical power to her personal sorrows: Hanaford, *Women of the Century,* p. 675. She gave over 125 speeches in 1874 and 1875.

8. Her "program": *St. Joseph Valley Register,* Apr. 16, 1874.

9. *Elkhart Observer* and other Elkhart newspapers, every issue from late March through June, 1874; see Note 4.

10. *Elkhart Observer,* Apr. 29, 1874. Shumard & Golden's was the focal point of Crusaders' gatherings in Elkhart.

11. Spring election campaign, *Elkhart Observer,* May 6, 1874; *Goshen Democrat,* May 13, 1874; *Elkhart Democratic Union,* May 8, 1874. Legal and political battles reported frequently in the *Elkhart Observer, Review, Democratic Union,* and *Goshen Democrat; Woman's Journal,* June 3, 1876. Hiring of Pinkerton detectives to catch Frank McKinistry is detailed by Emma (or Edward?) Molloy in "A Band of Desperadoes," *Chicago Inter-Ocean,* Dec. 18, 1874.

12. Suit: *Goshen Democrat,* May 20, 1874. County convention in Elkhart County: *Elkhart Observer,* June 24, 1874.

13. "On the Road," *Elkhart Observer,* July 1, 1874.

14. *Goshen Democrat,* Aug. 5, 1874; *Elkhart Observer,* Aug. 19, 1874.

15. Her role at the first Indiana WCTU convention: WCTU of Indiana, Minutes, p. 16, 27-33 (Indiana Division, Indiana State Library); *Indianapolis Journal,* Sept. 2-4, 1874.

16. For accounts of WCTU at Indiana General Assembly see *Indianapolis Journal* and *Sentinel,* Jan. 22, 1875; Frances E. Willard Scrapbook 5, Temperance and Prohibition Papers, WCTU Series, Sec. II, Roll 30, p. 249. Zerelda Wallace (1817-1901), widow of Gov. David Wallace, stepmother of Lew Wallace, worked for woman suffrage in Indiana, headed the National WCTU's Franchise Dept. and was president of the Indiana WCTU Account of her "conversion" to female suffrage in *Our Union,* Aug. 15, 1880, p. 1-2 (at Frances E. Willard Library, Evanston); *LaPorte Herald-Chronicle,* Apr. 22, 1880.

17. Remarks at American Woman Suffrage Association convention, *Woman's Journal,* Dec. 4, 1875, p. 386-87.

Chapter 7

1. The *Goshen Democrat* especially opposed Emma Molloy during the Crusade. Her

problems with the WCTU in its earliest years: *Indianapolis Journal*, June 11, 12, 1875; *Woman's Journal*, July 1, 1876, p. 209; *ibid.*, Jan. 6, 1877, p. 8.

2. Her close ties with the WCTU included service in several states and attending national conventions in 1876, 1879, 1884, and 1894. A major contribution in Indiana was serving as state organizer in 1880.

3. Tippecanoe rally described in *Elkhart Observer*, Aug. 19, Sept. 19, 1874.

4. Chapters she organized are listed in *Proceedings of 21st Session, Indiana Grand Lodge I.O.G.T...*(Indianapolis, 1875), p. 53-54; *Proceedings of 22nd Session...*(Indianapolis, 1876), p. 54-55 (Indiana Division, Indiana State Library). The *Advance Guard* has not been located; referred to in Indiana WCTU, Minutes, p. 86; *Proceedings, 21st Annual Session...I.O.G.T.*, p. 8; *Elkhart Observer*, July 14, 1875.

5. Letters in *Elkhart Observer*, July 1, 22, Sept. 16, 1874. Article in *Chicago Inter-Ocean*, Aug. 27, 1875. *Observer* issues Sept. 1, 1875 - April 1876 are not available, except Mar. 22, 1876 (at American Antiquarian Society).

6. "Emma's Effusion," *Fort Wayne News*, Mar. 3, 1886.

7. Succeful women often downplayed their ambitions: Carolyn G. Heilbrun, *Writing a Woman's Life* (New York, 1988), p. 22-25.

8. Edward Molloy's coldness toward a male friend of his wife, c. 1880-81, described in *Wabash* (Indiana) *Courier*, June 30, 1882. Among the men she worked with in the first years were J. J. Talbott (Indiana), Rev. George A. Vibbert (Massachusetts), Addington Welch (Rhode Island), and Henry Waldo Adams (New York). There is no definite evidence today that she engaged in love affairs with any of the men she met in her work, but during her lifetime and after, there were many rumors and accusations. Her "confession" of a love affair between herself and Talbott was one of the plausible-sounding but unprovable accounts by her later friend, the alleged murderer George Graham, in *Springfield* (Missouri) *Express*, Apr. 20, 1886.

9. Her Woman's Congress address in *Woman's Journal*, Nov. 28, 1874, p. 380; meeting description, *Elkhart Observer*, Oct. 21, 18, Nov. 4, 1874. AWSA convention: *Woman's Journal*, Dec. 4, 1875, p. 386-87; Woman Suffrage Association of Indiana, Minutes, Nov. 24, 1875 (Indiana Historical Society Library). She was twice elected a vice president of the WSAI (Minutes, May 26, 1875, May 30, 1876).

10. Emma's work in Massachusetts was frequently mentioned in *Woman's Journal*, May-July 1876; in Massachusetts newspapers that spring and fall; in *Annual Report, Massachusetts Temperance Alliance...1876*, p. 146; in *Annual Report, Massachusetts Total Abstinence Society...1876*, p. 4 (at Boston Public Library). The *National Temperance Advocate*, May 1876, p. 80, refers inquiries about her to the Lyceum Bureau, Boston. Speech to New England Woman Suffrage Association: *Woman's Journal*, June 3, 1876, p. 184; June 10, 1876, p. 188. Her remarks to the International Temperance Conference in *Centennial Temperance Volume...*(New York, 1877), p. 150-51; her report on the Centennial: *Woman's Journal*, July 1, 1876, p. 209.

11. Sale of *Observer*: *Goshen Democrat*, Apr. 5, 12, 1876. Moving: *Indianapolis Journal*, May 4, 1876. Edward Molloy's move to *LaPorte Chronicle* (later *Herald-Chronicle*): *South Bend Tribune*, May 3, 1878.

12. Change noted in *Elkhart Sentinel*, Mar. 6, 1886; *Ribbon Workers*, p. 301-02; *Spokane Spokesman-Review*, Jan. 15, 1896.

13. Francis Murphy (1836-1907) was the most famed of the gospel temperance orators. Emma's Ribbon work is described with many anecdotes in Hiatt, *Ribbon Workers*, p. 294-304, as well as newspapers wherever she visited. She maintained her independence in the Ribbon movement, conducting her own campaigns, seeking local WCTU and clergy sup-

port.

14. Death of Talbott: *South Bend Tribune*, Sept. 2, 1876; *Ribbon Workers*, p. 301-02; *New Albany Ledger-Standard*, Sept. 6, 1876. Talbott was accused of taking funds from the state organization: *Proceedings of the 22nd Session of the Grand Lodge of Indiana, I.O.G.T.* (Indianapolis, 1876), p. 7-9.

15. Emma's Vermont work is described by Deborah P. Clifford in "The Women's War Against Rum," *Vermont History*, v. LII (Summer, 1984), p. 153-54; in Vermont papers, including the *Burlington Free Press* and *Vermont Christian Messenger* (Montpelier); in *Woman's Journal*, Mar. 17, 1877, p. 85 and Mar. 31, 1877, p. 97. She claimed 2,300 pledges as of mid-March (*Burlington Free Press*, Mar. 14, 1877). She attended a Maine WCTU convention: *Our Union*, Mar. 1877, p. 4. Her articles appeared in *Indianapolis Journal*, Jan. 24, Feb. 20, 1877.

16. Founding of South Bend Reform Club: Chapman, *History of St. Joseph County*, p. 585; *South Bend Tribune*, Apr. 4-23, 1877. *Tribune* quotes: Apr. 9, 11, 1877. For some time Emma kept in touch with the club. Chapman's notes that after a "lull," it was revived by others in the summer of 1878.

17. Talbott had been among the seceders in the Good Templars' split, following the lead of British members in 1876. Her brief account of Portland meeting: *South Bend Tribune*, May 29, 1877. Her alleged role behind the scenes at Portland is described by an opponent in *Templar/Temperance Journal* (UK.), Dec. 18, 1878, p. 386. Telegram to Lucy Hayes, May 23, 1877, Lucy Webb Hayes Correspondence (Hayes Presidential Center Library).

18. Her 1878 campaign: *Woman's Journal*, Apr. 13, 1878, p. 120; Massachusetts newspapers; *Annual Report, Massachusetts Temperance Alliance*, 1878, p. 5; *ibid.*, 1879, p. 9; *Crusade* (UK.), Feb. 1879, p. 8. In the *Woman's Journal* article a total of 125,000 pledges was claimed. A sketch in *Good Templars' Watchword* (UK.), Oct. 9, 1878, claimed 100,000 pledges since Jan. 1. Massachusetts State House visit: *Our Union*, Dec. 1878, p. 3. Address to New England Woman Suffrage Association: *Woman's Journal*, June 1, 1878, p. 172. World Good Templars meeting: *International Good Templar* (UK.), No. 3, 1878, p. 63-78.

19. Receptions: *South Bend Tribune*, June 1, 1878, *Woman's Journal*, Sept. 21, 1878, p. 302. Livermore: see Ch. 5, note 14.

20. *Ballot Box*, Nov., 1877, p. 1.

Chapter 8

1. It should be noted that Emma was not alone among American temperance workers in visiting England. Notable among them were Frances E. Willard and the orator John B. Gough. Her work in Ratcliff Highway, London, 1878 described in *Temperance Cause*, Dec. 15, 1878, p. 27; *East London Observer*, Nov. 9, 1878; *Good Templars' Watchword*, Oct. 16, 30, 1888; *Alliance News*, Nov. 9, 1878, and others. American sources on her English work include *Woman's Journal*, Nov. 9, 1878, p. 351; Nov. 30, 1878, p. 381; Jan. 18, 1879, p. 17; the *Temperance Cause*, Nov. 15, 1878, p. 1, Dec. 15, 1878, p. 1 (American Antiquarian Society). British temperance journals: *Good Templars' Watchword*, Oct. 2, 1878-Jan. 22, 1879 (every issue); *Alliance News*, Oct. 19, 1878, p. 660, Nov. 9, 1878, p. 726, Dec. 7, 1878, p. 780; *Templar and Temperance Journal*, Sept. 25, 1878, p. 197, Dec. 18, 1878, p. 386; *Christian World*, Dec. 6, 1878, p. 961; *The Crusade*, Feb. 1879, p. 8-9; and British newspapers (at British Library).

2. *Meyers' Enfield Observer and Local and General Advertiser*, Nov. 23, 1878.

3. *Hackney & Kingsland Gazette and Shoreditch Telegraph*, Oct. 21, 1878. In this same

talk, Emma spoke of knowing a "great naturalist" who described a dangerous climb in which, unknown to him, his little boy had followed him.

4. Accident described in *Good Templars' Watchword,* Dec. 18, 1878, p. 833. Portrait: *ibid.,* Jan. 22, 1878, p. 56.

5. Her recuperation is described in *South Bend Tribune,* Jan. 31, 1879. Her further work in New England: *ibid.,* Mar. 8, 31; *Woman's Journal,* Apr. 12, 1879, p. 113; Oct. 4, 1879, p. 320; *Providence Journal,* Mar. 18, 1879; many Massachusetts newspapers; *Temperance Cause,* Apr. 15, 1879, p. 59; May 15, 1879, p. 69; Sept. 15, 1879, p. 98; *National Temperance Advocate,* Sept. 1879, p. 140 (Boston Public Library). Success of her voter registration speeches: *Woman's Journal,* Oct. 4, 1879, p. 320.

6. First notice of her work on the *Morning and Day Reform* found in *Woman's Journal,* Apr. 12, 1879, p. 113; *Temperance Cause,* Apr. 15, 1879, p. 59; *South Bend Tribune,* Apr. 26, 1879. Unfortunately, just a few issues of this once widely circulated journal (1874-1885) have been found, at the American Antiquarian Society, Kansas State Historical Society, University of Kansas Library, and Washington County, Kansas Historical Society. Additional clipped articles and pages, including articles by Emma Molloy, are in Frances Willard Scrapbooks 5, 7, 9, 11, 12, 14, 17 (Temperance and Prohibition Papers, WCTU Series); a few articles are reprinted in the *Christian Worker* (Earlham College Archives). Missing issues could shed much light on Emma Molloy's work and relationships with other temperance figures.

7. Emma's lengthy account of the reunion: "A Family Camp-Meeting," *Livingston Republican,* Geneseo, New York, July 3, 1879.

8. Party: *South Bend Tribune,* July 19, 1879.

9. Gospel temperance revivals assisted by Rebecca Trego noted in *LaPorte Herald-Chronicle,* May 19, 1881; *Topeka Capital,* Feb. 22, 1881. Revivalism also may have been a more appealing approach than temperance in some places.

10. *Indianapolis Journal,* Nov. 1, 1879, *Evansville Journal,* May 17, 1880.

11. Move to LaPorte: *South Bend Tribune,* Mar. 31, 1880. Indiana prison work is described in *Woman's Journal,* July 12, 1879, p. 122; *Christian Worker,* Aug. 11, 1881, p. 382; *LaPorte Herald-Chronicle,* June 17, 1880. Membership on committee: *Our Union,* Dec. 1879, p. 13.

12. The *Indianapolis Journal,* Feb. 13, Mar. 15, 1880, has long accounts of two Ex-Convicts' Aid Society meetings with Coffin, Gov. Hendricks, and ex-Gov. Baker, among others, as speakers. Emma promoted it at the state WCTU convention: *Evansville Journal,* May 14, 1880; Minutes, Indiana WCTU, p. 192. More information on this movement could not be found, but *Minutes of the National WCTU Convention, 1880,* p. 126, call it "among the most successful" of its kind by the WCTU.

13. *Indianapolis Journal,* Aug. 4, 1879.

14. Sources on her early work in Kansas are Topeka and Leavenworth newspapers; *Kansas Temperance Palladium,* 1880; *W.C.T.U. of Kansas, Minutes of the Third Annual Meeting* (Topeka, 1881), p. 13 (all at the Kansas State Historical Society). Her work included both temperance revivals and pressure for enactment of, or compliance with, law. Her correspondence with St. John, from Feb. 1, 1881, is in the Gov. John P. St. John Papers, Kansas State Historical Society.

15. The Grand Temperance Council's efforts are summarized in Gayle Thornbrough, *Indiana in the Civil War Era* (Indianapolis, 1966), p. 265; Charles E. Canup, "The Temperance Movement in Indiana," *Indiana Magazine of History,* v. XVI (June, 1916), p. 120-28; Harold C. Feightner, *Wet and Dry Legislation in Indiana,* p. 75-87 (Indiana Division, Indiana

State Library). Indiana newspapers followed its progress, as did the anti-temperance *Journal of Freedom and Right,* 1879-81 (Indiana State Library), and *Christian Worker, Western Christian Advocate,* and *Our Union.*

16. The St. John papers contain correspondence with Emma Molloy and several other Indiana workers. Her organizing for the Indiana WCTU: *Evansville Journal,* May 14-15, 1880; *Our Union,* April 1, 1880, p. 5; June 15, 1880, p. 5; Dec. 1, 1880, p. [11-12]. *Liquor Dealers' Gospel No. 2* is in the Indiana Historical Society Library. Data prepared by the Council is in the Indiana Division, Indiana State Library. Her work is described in *Indianapolis Sentinel,* Feb. 5, 1880; *South Bend Tribune,* Mar. 6, 1880; *Journal of Freedom and Right,* Feb. 26, 1880, Jan. 7, 1881; *Kokomo Dispatch,* Mar. 4, 25, 1880, June 2, 20, Oct. 6, 1881; *Rochester Republican,* July 15, 1880. Her article against foreigners reprinted in *Christian Worker,* Jan. 27, 1881, p. 45. The LaPorte rally described in *LaPorte Herald-Chronicle,* July 28-Sept. 1, 1881, and in a diary of ex-Gov. Neal Dow of Maine, 1879-81, Neal Dow Papers (at the Neal Dow Memorial, Portland, Maine). Woman suffrage amendment: Janice M. LaFlamme, *Strategy of Feminine Protest...*(Bloomington, 1968) (Indiana Division, Indiana State Library).

17. Election: Indiana WCTU Minutes, p. 234. Emma's article: "The Women in Council," from the *Morning and Day of Reform,* in Frances E. Willard scrapbook 11, p. 20-21, Temperance and Prohibition Papers, WCTU Series, Reel 31, p. 232, 236-37. St. John's letter edited by Willard: *Our Union,* Dec. 1881, p. 15.

Chapter 9

1. Divorce: La Porte County, Indiana Circuit Court Record, Roll 6, Cause 11854. The elder Molloys listed in U S. Census, LaPorte County, Indiana, 1880, p. 192. The inevitable bitterness of the divorce experience apparently mellowed. In later years she wrote, "...we are excellent friends. If he has ever expressed himself to any one detrimental to me, or as jealous of me, I have never heard it." (*Springfield Express,* May 14, 1886.)

2. An outline of her life, 1882-86, is given in *The Graham Tragedy and the Molloy-Lee Examination* (Springfield, Missouri, 1886), p. 14-18, 44-45, 110 (at the State Historical Society of Missouri, Columbia); *Springfield Express,* Mar. 26, May 14, 1886. There are references to illness in various newspaper accounts, mostly unspecified but including nervous headache. See also Chapter 5, Note 17.

3. There is a regrettable lack of information on Emma's relationship with Frank and Etta. There may possibly have been a family connection between the Lee girls and a Molloy friend (see Notes on Emma's Family). Cora had sewn for Emma (*The Graham Tragedy,* p. 110). In Elgin, Cora and Sarah Graham opened a dressmaking shop (*Elgin Daily News,* Aug. 28, 1883). Ida Lee worked at the publishing house (*ibid.,* Feb. 25, 1883), as did Etta (*Elgin City Directory,* 1884-85). Ida married William Dixon of Nebraska (*Springfield Express,* Nov. 11, 1887). Cora became Cora Juel and lived in Auburn, Nebraska.

4. *Leavenworth Times,* July 8, 1882. Other articles, *ibid.,* July 6-7, 11-14, 18, 1882.

5. Her prison work at Leavenworth (perhaps the state prison) is described in an undated clipping in Scrapbook 14, Gov. John P. St. John Papers. It gives Emma's account of writing a prisoner's mother. She was said to have found jobs for 200-300 ex-prisoners from various prisons: *Springfield* (Missouri) *Express,* June 17, 1887. Work in the Colorado state prison mentioned in *Pacific Christian Advocate,* Apr. 28, 1887.

6. Newspapers mentioning her work in this drive include *Ohio Liberal,* Mansfield, Ohio, Aug. 29, Sept. 19, 26, 1883 (Ohio Historical Society); *Union Signal,* Oct. 30, 1884, p. 19.

7. *Cherokee Advocate,* Tahlequah, Oklahoma, Dec. 14, 1883. Her work with Cherokees

in *Union Signal,* Feb. 21, 1884, p. 11; Mar. 6, 1884, p. 9; May 29, 1884, p. 12; Jan. 8, 1885, p. 13; *Cherokee Advocate,* Dec. 7, 14, 21, 1883; Jan. 4, 11, 18, May 16, 23, 30, 1884; *Elgin News,* Dec. 22, 1883; *Washington* (Kansas) *Republican,* Apr. 25, 1884; Elizabeth Ross, "WCTU Cherokee Nation," Mss. #7401, *W.P.A. Indian and Pioneer History,* Vol. 43 (at Oklahoma Historical Society); Rev. Edmund Schwarze, *History of the Moravian Missions Among Southern Indian Tribes . . .* (Bethlehem, Pa., 1928), p. 301. It should be noted that Emma was not the only female temperance worker who visited the Cherokees.

8. *Ibid.,* Jan. 11, 1884. Emma's taking Frank with her: *Elgin Frank,* Dec. 29, 1883.

9. *Western Brewer,* v. IX No. 2, Feb. 15, 1884, p. 277 (Anheuser-Busch Library, St. Louis).

10. *Wabash Courier,* June 23, 30, July 7, 14, 18, 1882; *Chicago Inter-Ocean,* June 24, 28, 1882; *Fort Wayne Sentinel,* June 26, 29, July 8, 1882. Accumulating a fortune was not possible in her work; she relied on a prior agreement to pay her expenses, or a collection taken the last day of her meetings. The *Western Brewer* chose to ignore most speakers as individuals, but blast them collectively.

11. *Morning and Day of Reform,* Aug. 1884, p. 3 (Kansas State Historical Society); *The Graham Tragedy,* p. 14-15, 44, 51-52, 63, 69, 75. The *Washington Republican* and *Washington County Register* note their activities. Her later Kansas work is described in the *Kansas Prohibitionist,* 1884, and various Kansas newspapers.

12. *Western Brewer,* v. IX #11, Nov. 15, 1884, p. 1931. Issues are delineated in *Kansas Prohibitionist,* July 23, 1884; her address to WCTU state convention, *Kansas Commoner,* Leavenworth, Oct. 25, 1884. The convention and Emma Molloy (in *Morning and Day of Reform,* July-Sept. 1884) backed Republicans for state office. The decline of the *Morning* is described in *Washington Republican,* Dec. 26, 1884, Jan. 9, Mar. 13, July 3, 1885; *Graham Tragedy,* p. 44. Graham noted subscriptions fell from 18,000 to 10,000. She made numerous appearances for the WCTU in Kansas and served as a district president: Minutes, 5th District, Kansas WCTU, 1885-1909, Mary Dobbs collection, Box 9 (Kansas State Historical Society); *Minutes, Sixth Annual Meeting, WCTU of Kansas...*(Fort Scott, 1884), p. 17, 18, 22, 25, 29, 50; *Union Signal,* Oct. 2, 1884, p. 11; Oct. 30, 1884, p. 12, 19, 21; *Washington Republican,* Oct. 24, 1884. It is possible that the journal already was in considerable decline when Emma took it over. Ill health was a reason given for selling the paper (*Woman's Tribune,* June, 1885).

13. Emma Molloy's and George Graham's movements before and during the trial are detailed in *The Graham Tragedy;* newspapers of Washington, Springfield, South Bend, Fort Wayne, Elkhart, Peoria, St. Louis, and others, including the *New York Times,* Apr. 3, 1887; and the *National Police Gazette.* Legal proceedings: Circuit Court records, Green and Christian Counties, Missouri. The case is still baffling today. So are Graham's writings, many of which appear to have truth in them. Emma reacted to the great stress with physical symptoms, including a convulsive attack (*Springfield Express,* Mar. 26, 1886). The press reported a suicide attempt (*Fort Wayne Daily News,* Mar. 23, 1886).

14. *Fort Wayne* (Indiana) *Gazette,* Apr. 1, 1886; *St. Joseph Valley Register,* reprinted in *Peoria Journal,* Mar. 5, 1886.

15. *Springfield* (Missouri) *Express,* May 14, 1886; *South Bend Tribune,* Apr. 27, 1886.

16. *Springfield Express,* Feb. 11, June 24, 1887; *Fort Wayne Gazette,* Feb. 8, 1887; *Puget Sound Argus,* Port Townsend, Washington, Feb. 2, 22, 1888.

17. Poem appeared in *Springfield Express,* Aug. 27, 1886. Account of drowning: *South Bend Tribune,* July 23-24, 1886; *South Bend Times,* July 23, 1886; *LaPorte Herald-Chronicle,*

July 29, 1886.

18. *South Bend Tribune,* July 26, 1886; *LaPorte Herald-Chronicle,* July 29, 1886.

19. *South Bend Tribune* and *South Bend Times,* Sept. 4, 1886; *Mishawaka Enterprise,* Sept. 10, 1886; *Elkhart Sentinel,* Sept. 11, 1886; *Springfield Express,* Sept. 10, 1886. According to the *Sentinel,* Emma nearly drowned. The *South Bend Tribune* did *not* describe the incident as a suicide attempt.

20. *Puget Sound Argus,* Apr. 7, 14, 28, May 26, 1887; *Pacific Christian Advocate,* Mar. 31, Apr. 7, 21, 28, 1887; "A Strange Story of Crime," *New York Times,* Apr. 3, 1887; *Portland Oregonian,* Mar. 22, 29, Apr. 1, 11, 1887, Jan. 21, 1888.

21. *Washington County* (Kansas) *Register,* Oct. 14, 1887; *Washington Post,* Oct. 12, 19, 1887; *Springfield Express,* Mar. 16, 1888. Responses of Mary Livermore: *Puget Sound Weekly Argus,* Jan. 7, 1887; Frances Willard: *ibid.,* Apr. 7, 1887; Indiana WCTU: Minutes, p. 413-14; James G. Clark: *Fort Wayne News,* May 10, 1886; Emile Cary: *ibid.,* May 10, 1886; Studebaker: *Springfield Express,* Mar. 9, 1888; Molloy: *Peoria Journal,* Mar. 5, 1886.

Chapter 10

1. Her statement: *Springfield Express,* Mar. 16, 1888. Her work at Port Townsend is described often in the *Port Townsend Leader* and *Pacific Christian Advocate,* and in Harriet L. Adams, *A Woman's Journey in the New Northwest* (Cleveland, 1892), p. 51. Seamen's Bethel preaching: *Port Townsend Daily Leader,* Oct. 27, 1889, June 18, 1890, May 13, 1891; entertainment: *ibid.,* Oct. 27, Nov. 7, 1889, July 5, 1891; finance: *ibid.,* Jan. 22, Aug. 23, 1890. WCTU: *ibid.,* June 2, Sept. 16, Oct. 15, 1892. Preaching at Methodist church: *ibid.,* June 1, Oct. 19, Dec. 31, 1890, Aug. 10, 1892, Jan. 13, 1895, Aug. 9, 1896. Accounts of her revival work in newspapers throughout the states/province mentioned; in the *Pacific Christian Advocate,* 1887-1900; and the *California Christian Advocate,* 1901-07. For awhile she edited a temperance column for the *Port Townsend Daily Leader* (as on Nov. 13, 1892). She also worked at least briefly on behalf of a Chautauqua University of the West.

2. Information from marriage notice, Linn County, Oregon, Marriage Book G, printed in *Pacific Christian Advocate,* Jan. 10, 1889, p. 8; obituary of Morris Barrett, *ibid.,* Feb. 11, 1903, p. 18. According to his obituary, Morris Barrett was first married to Kate Kilpatrick; she was the mother of his son Clarence. This account describes her as "an adopted daughter of William Seward." A Fred Seward recommended Clarence for early appointments, according to Federal personnel records on Barrett. Emma and Morris' life together described in Adams, *A Woman's Journey,* p. 51. House: *Puget Sound Weekly Argus,* Aug. 30, Sept. 27, Nov. 15, 1888. Adams' visit: *Port Townsend Daily Leader,* Oct. 22, Nov. 21, 1890. Daniel Dale: *ibid.,* June 21, 1891. Another example of Emma's aid to the unfortunate (transporting five motherless children of a blind father): *ibid.,* Nov. 3, 1892.

3. Illnesses included influenza (*Port Townsend Daily Leader,* Jan. 31, 1892, *Pacific Christian Advocate,* Feb. 13, 1901); seizure while preaching (see Chapter 5, Note 17). Item on Olympia, *Pacific Christian Advocate,* Apr. 5, 1893, May 10, 1893; Everett, *ibid.,* June 28, 1893; Spokane, *ibid.,* Mar. 27, 1895.

Some other revivals in Washington: LaCamas, Vancouver, East Sound, Seattle, Dungeness, Port Hadlock, Kent, South Bend, Shelton. In Oregon: Baker City, Eugene, Salem, Halsey, Harrisburg, Roseburg, Ashland, Portland, Long Creek, Grants Pass, Pendleton, Marshfield,

Forest Grove, Cottage Grove, Sheridan, Hillsboro, Webfoot, Dayton, McMinnville, LaGrande. In British Columbia: Vancouver, New Westminster, Sidney. In California: Lower Lake, Los Gatos, Kelseyville, Peachland, Forestville, Fairfield, Santa Cruz, Petaluma, Oak Park, Healdsburg, Vacaville, Valley Spring, Point Richmond, Ione, Oakland, Auburn, Elk Grove, Sutter City, Ukiah, Occidental, San Jose, Morgan Hill, Sacramento, Gilroy, Santa Clara, Susanville, Cedarville. In Nevada: Winnemucca. Etta married Decatur Blakeney Nov. 28, 1888 (marriage certificate, Jefferson County, Washington, Jan. 2, 1889). Morris may have accompanied Emma on some trips. The Barretts traveled East together in 1893 to visit family (*Port Townsend Daily Leader,* Aug. 23-24, 1893).

    4. *Vancouver Daily World,* Nov. 22, 1890.

    5. *Spokane Spokesman-Review,* Jan. 20, 1896.

    6. *Vancouver Daily World,* Nov. 22, 1890. Robert Ingersoll (1833-99) was a well-known agnostic lecturer.

    7. Stroke mentioned in Morris Barrett obituary. Foster daughter Bessie: Federal Census, Jefferson County, Washington, 1900, p. 121.

    8. Amity account in *Pacific Christian Advocate,* Nov. 30, 1904, p. 15-16. Yuba City: *Sutter County Farmer,* Yuba City, California, Mar. 30, 1906.

    9. Obituaries: *Journal of the California Annual Conference,* 1907, p. 59; *Port Townsend Leader,* May 15, 1907; *South Bend Times* and *South Bend Tribune,* May 15, 1907. In a story passed down to descendants of Etta Molloy Blakeney, as related by Jean Hass, Emma at some point seemed to "rise from the dead" — perhaps coming out of a coma for a time.

    10. *Port Townsend Weekly Leader,* May 29, 1907.

    11. Jefferson County, Washington, Record of Wills, Vol. B, p. 42. Except for her correspondence with St. John, none of her known personal papers have been located. They do appear to have been destroyed, as instructed in her will, by her friend and executor, John M. Lockhart. His descendant, when asked, believed this to be the case. The papers may have included Emma's correspondence, old letters of her mother's she had saved, household and trip diaries, and autograph books including temperance pledge records, among other items. Her book manuscript, "A History of the St. Joseph Country," also is unaccounted for. She may have begun her autobiography. Her father also was said to have kept a diary (he lived until 1899).

    12. Information on the memorial window is from a 1976 bulletin of Trinity United Methodist Church, Port Townsend.

    13. Edward Molloy: obituary, *Indiana Magazine of History,* v. X, p. 88; *LaPorte Herald,* Mar. 18, 1914.

Chapter 11

    1. *South Bend Tribune,* May 10, 1877.

    2. *Spokane Spokesman-Review,* Jan. 25, 1896.

    3. *Fort Wayne News,* Mar. 3, 1886.

Writings and Addresses

    1. This was an actual girls' college in southeastern Alabama. Its records could not be located.

2. Probably based on the *New York Ledger*, a popular newspaper that was famed for its "matrimonial" advertising.

3. Refers to literary or song characters of the day.

4. Some of this information also fits Louis Pradt.

5. A real person, "Brick" Pomeroy was a well-known Wisconsin journalist. It is possible that Emma may have met him.

6. Popular Scottish poet Robert Burns.

7. Short for "Kuzzin Mehitable."

8. *Wisconsin State Journal.*

9. S. O. Raymond.

10. Jackson Hadley.

11. "A bill to amend the cemetery law to allow the Milwaukee Chamber of Commerce to authorize a private cemetery to remain at St. John's parsonage," *Wisconsin Daily Capitol,* Mar. 9, 1866.

12. Slang for "ten drinks."

13. Vilas House Hotel, corner Main St. & Wisconsin Ave.

14. W. H. Chandler.

15. A machine-made lace collar with patterned leaves, flowers, etc., named for lacemakers in Honiton, Devonshire, England.

16. Thomas Carlyle, English writer much read at the time.

17. From the well-known poem, "A Psalm of Life," by Henry Wadsworth Longfellow.

18. Irwin and Erastus Beadle's "dime novels" were immensely popular with soldiers during the Civil War.

19. Jones's Wood, a 160-acre park bounded roughly by Third Avenue, the East River, 66th St. and 75th St., was favored by German immigrants. The Molloys were attending the Soldiers and Sailors Convention. Other events, deleted from this excerpt: a performance by the "Worrell sisters" (whom Emma knew) and a ballet, "The White Fawn"; conversations with Civil War veterans, and visits to Coney Island, St. Stephen's Church, and Cypress Hills, a Jewish cemetery where two young people drowned in an accident in South Bend were buried.

20. Edward Molloy; Emma often uses this Irish nickname.

21. The Rev. Horace Bushnell, a prominent Methodist preacher and author, wrote "Woman Suffrage: The Reform Against Nature" in 1869 (*Dictionary of American Biography,* v. II, p. 352).

22. Reformers Elizabeth Cady Stanton and Mary Livermore.

23. Alexander Turney Stewart, a New York millionaire and civic leader, owned the largest dry goods store in the world. The Fifth Avenue home of the Stewarts was considered America's finest mansion *(Dictionary of American Biography,* v. IX, p. 3-4).

24. A domestic worker who aided the Molloys. She is mentioned frequently in the column.

25. Jane Grey Swisshelm (1815-84), a pioneering woman journalist, opened the press gallery of Congress to women. Her trail-blazing political journalism may have inspired Emma. Emma could easily have met Swisshelm in Madison in 1862, when Swisshelm visited there to speak on "Woman in Politics," and appeared before the state legislature: *Wisconsin Daily Patriot,* Feb. 19, 1862; Diary of Emilie Quiner, Feb. 20, 1862 (Wisconsin State Historical Society). Helen Wood Manville of LaCrosse, Wisconsin, whom Emma might also have known, wrote under the name "Nellie A. Mann" (*National Cyclopedia of American Biography,* v. 4, 523). Dr. Ellen Ferguson could not be identified. An Ellen Ferguson was active in the Woman Suffrage Association of Indiana.

26. Typesetting terms. Before typesetting machines, each letter was placed by hand in a "form" or frame.

27. Journeyman printers, relied upon for typesetting and running the press, had high rates of alcoholism. Many known as "tramp printers" traveled from town to town.

28. Possibly the lengthy scandal involving the Rev. Henry Ward Beecher's involvement with Mrs. Theodore Tilton.

29. "Printer's devil," a boy who did various jobs in the newspaper or printer's office.

30. Probably refers to the Interstate Industrial Exposition, begun in Chicago in 1873 and held annually thereafter.

31. Editor of the *North Iowa Times*, earlier of South Bend, who published many of Emma's early writings.

32. Schuyler Colfax, who rose to become Vice President (1868-72), founded and published the *St. Joseph Valley Register.*

33. May refer to Mrs. Caroline A. Soule, a temperance worker from New York, who shared the platform with Emma at a temperance meeting in Chicago in 1874 (Frances Willard Scrapbook 4, p. 14, Temperance and Prohibition Papers).

34. Son Franklin Molloy; adopted daughter Etta Molloy.

35. Refers to an episode of the Woman's Temperance Crusade in Chicago in Mar. 1874.

36. Senator Charles Sumner, uncompromising abolitionist.

37. For a description of the Blue Ribbon movement in England and Booth's role, see Lillian L. Shiman, *The Crusade Against Drink in Victorian England* (New York, 1988), p. 109-121.

38. Adeline Dutton Train Whitney (1824-1906) was a prolific and popular American writer of moralistic popular fiction and verse (*Notable American Women*, v. III, p. 599).

39. J. K. Osgood of Gardiner, Maine began the movement in 1872.

40. Francis Murphy, the famed temperance evangelist, was featured in articles in the *Morning and Day of Reform* while Emma served as writer/assistant editor.

41. Cyrus Sturdevant (*The True Path; or Gospel Temperance . . ..* J. F. Banks, Chicago 1878, p. 419).

42. Dr. Henry A. Reynolds of Bangor, Maine, began organizing Reform Clubs (Red Ribbon) in Maine in 1874 (*Cyclopedia of Temperance & Prohibition,* Funk & Wagnalls, N. Y., 1891, p. 57).

43. William Noble, who began the Ribbon movement in England, was inspired by Francis Murphy while visiting the United States. (*Cyclopedia of Temperance & Prohibition,* p. 360.)

44. Two infamous Confederate prisons during the Civil War.

45. Probably refers to Charles Forbes Rene de Montealembert (1810-70), a Catholic liberal politician in Europe (*New Catholic Encyclopedia,* v. 9, p. 1074).

46. Emma shared the lecture platform with the great reformer (1811-84) on occasion. In 1878 he signed her testimonial and wrote a letter on her behalf to British reformers.

47. Prohibitionist party backed by the WCTU in 1884.

48. Maj. Gen. James B. Steedman lost 49% of his troops in less than four hours at the battle of Chickamauga (James Longstreet, *From Manassas to Appomattox,* Bloomington 1960, p. 459).

49. Emma apparently never published her autobiography.

50. Judge James Baker of Springfield, Missouri.

Emma's Family

1. Barrett and Bosworth family histories; Barrett data, Milo B. Howard papers, Alabama Department of Archives and History; South Bend City Cemetery records; obituaries of Susannah Newton Hackney (*South Bend Tribune,* June 6, 1874); William L. Barrett (*South Bend Times,* Mar. 29, 1899); Harriett Eaker Barrett *(ibid.,* Apr. 11, 1898); Zilpha Barrett Hogue and William E. Barrett (family scrapbook, J. Barrett Guthrie; Zilpha's death date mentioned in William Barrett obituary, South Bend City Cemetery records); John C. Barrett (*South Bend Tribune* Feb. 28, 1940); May Barrett (*ibid.,* Feb. 21, 1942); year of Edward Barrett's death given in William L. Barrett's sketch in *South Bend and the Men Who Have Made It;* Edward Molloy (*LaPorte Herald,* Mar. 18, 1914); Morris Barrett (*Pacific Christian Advocate,* Feb. 11, 1903); Lottie Pradt (*Wisconsin State Journal,* Oct. 24, 1863); Allie Pradt *(ibid.,* Aug. 18, 1864); Franklin Molloy *(South Bend Times,* July 23, 1886). According to her obituary, Lottie Pradt was originally buried in Madison, but at some point apparently the remains were brought to South Bend City Cemetery. Clarence Barrett: U.S. Census, Columbus, Ohio 1900, v. 54 ED 125 Sheet 7. Descendants of Etta Molloy Blakeney: information comes from Jean Hass, Etta's great-granddaughter. Cora Juel's mother was Amanda (Lee) Manson (US. Census, Auburn, Nebraska, 1900, v. 29 E. D. 91, Sheet 11). A possible relationship to the Molloys' friend, Maj. Gen. M. D. Manson, has not yet been established.

The Ribbon Workers

1. Indiana was still part of the "West" in 1878.

2. May refer to Charles Taze Russell, a persuasive writer and preacher who founded the Watch Tower Bible and Tract Society.

3. John B. Gough, a noted lecturer, a native of England who had emigrated to America, was in England giving temperance speeches at the time Emma was there in 1878.

4. Eighteenth-century English philosopher John Locke and poet Alexander Pope.

5. Emma was married in her teens, but was not a mother until the age of twenty. (See text.)

6. Although it may well be that Louis Pradt had died before Emma began lecturing, he had not died at the time she left him and returned to South Bend (1867), since she divorced him that year. (See Chapter 4, Note 1.)

7. Emma's marriage to Edward Molloy came in 1867.

8. This is misleading. Emma Molloy first spoke formally before the public in 1870, on the subject of "Woman."

9. During the Elkhart Crusaders' prayer vigils outside Shumard and Golden's saloon, opposed by hecklers, in 1874, Isabel Henry, the widow of an Elkhart physican, was struck by a box. Her injury became a rallying point for the women.

10. Emma first lectured in Boston in the spring of 1876.

11. The Friendly-Inn may have been a temperance hotel. No information could be found on it or on Jennie McMasters.

12. Lydia and Phoebe were converts to Christianity in St. Paul's time; Phebe of Cenchrea is mentioned in Romans 16, Lydia of Thyatira, Macedonia, in Acts 16.

13. These were active suffrage/temperance workers. That summer the state's Prohibitionists would endorse woman suffrage. John I. Baker of Beverly, a longtime legislator, be-

came their nominee for Governor. In September the woman suffragists, acting as a political party, also nominated him.

14. Faxon (1823-1905), a merchant and temperance reformer, was responsible for landmark legislation in 1881.

15. Brown (1807-1890), a pioneering scientist/educator, was prominent in Indiana temperance work. He addressed the Indiana WCTU in June, 1875 on the disease nature of alcoholism.

16. Vibbert crusaded for both prohibition and woman suffrage, introducing a woman suffrage bill in 1871. He promoted the Prohibitionist ticket in 1876. Emma worked with him often.

17. John I. Baker (See Note 13) was joined by the Rev. Daniel Clarke Eddy as Prohibitionist candidate for lieutenant governor in 1876. According to *Woman's Journal* (Nov. 18, 1876, p. 372) they got 12,103 votes. Republican A. H. Rice was re-elected.

CREDITS

1. Writings/Addresses

"Answering An Advertisement" and "The Old Home," *North Iowa Times,* McGregor, Iowa; found at State Historical Society of Iowa, Iowa City.

"Soul-Clouds and Soul-Light" and "New Year's Eve," *Wisconsin Patriot,* and "Polly Wiggins Letter," *Wisconsin Capitol,* at State Historical Society of Wisconsin, Madison.

"The Insincerity of Social Life," advertisement for housekeeper, and "Our First Visit to New York," *South Bend National Union,* Northern Indiana Historical Society, South Bend.

"About Women," "The Housekeeper's Diary," and "A Question Answered," *Elkhart Observer,* Elkhart County Historical Society, Bristol, Indiana.

"Female Journalism" and address on temperance/woman suffrage, *Woman's Journal,* microfilm edition.

"The Blue Ribbon Brigade," *Good Templars' Watchword,* British Library, Colindale, U. K.

Decoration Day address and poem, *South Bend Tribune,* microfilm edition, St. Joseph County Public Library, South Bend, Indiana. (Original at Mishawaka-Penn Public Library, Mishawaka.)

Temperance address, *Kansas Commoner* (Leavenworth), Kansas State Historical Society, Topeka.

Self-defense from *Springfield Express,* State Historical Society of Missouri, Columbia.

"The Ministry of Love," *Pacific Christian Advocate,* microfilm edition.

2. Illustrations

Emma Molloy, c. 1876-77, and South Bend street scene (c. 1860): Northern Indiana Historical Society, South Bend.

William L. Barrett: Anderson and Cooley, *South Bend and the Men Who Have Made It* (Tribune Printing Co., South Bend, 1901), p. 239.

Other Barrett family members and Barrett houses: collection of J. Barrett Guthrie, San Juan Capistrano, California, a grandson of John C. ("Tony") Barrett, Emma's half-brother.

Edward Molloy: from an Indiana Civil War album at the Indiana Division, Indiana

State Library, Indianapolis.

Edward and Emma Molloy advertisement: photograph by *South Bend Tribune* from *Turner's South Bend Directory, 1871-72* (T. G. Turner, South Bend), p. 158, at Northern Indiana Historical Society, South Bend.

Barrett store sign: photo by the *South Bend Tribune.* Item at the Northern Indiana Historical Society.

Elkhart post office and newspaper office: photograph by Marion Troyer of an item at the Elkhart County Historical Society, Bristol, Indiana.

Robert K. Brush: from the personal collection of his great-great-grandson, the Rev. George M. Minnix, Elkhart, Indiana.

Engraving of Emma Molloy in *Good Templars' Watchword*: The British Library, Colindale, U. K.

Molloy-Graham home at Washington, Kansas: photograph by Mary Alice Pacey, historian, Washington County Historical Society.

Springfield Herald booklet, *The Graham Tragedy and the Molloy-Lee Examination*: State Historical Society of Missouri, Columbia.

Trinity Methodist Church: recent photograph furnished by the Rev. Dorothy Johnson, pastor, Trinity United Methodist Church, Port Townsend, Washington.

Emma Molloy Barrett at about fifty-five: *California Christian Advocate,* April 10, 1902, p. 13, at the United Library of Garrett Evangelical and Seabury-Western Theological Seminaries, Evanston, Illinois.

Emma Molloy Barrett at about sixty-five: from Jean Hass, Creswell, Oregon, great-granddaughter of Emma's adopted daughter, De'Etta Molloy Blakeney.

Tombstone: photograph by Eileen Martin, Port Townsend, Washington.

INDEX